Every Woman Has a Story

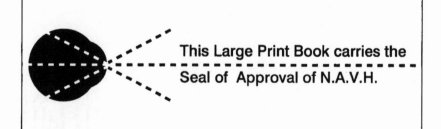

This Large Print Book carries the
Seal of Approval of N.A.V.H.

Every

Many Voices

Woman

Many Lessons

Has a

Many Lives

Story

True Tales compiled by

DARYL OTT UNDERHILL

G.K. Hall & Co. • Thorndike, Maine

Published in 1999 by arrangement with Warner Books, Inc.

G.K. Hall Large Print Core Series.

The text of this Large Print edition is unabridged.
Other aspects of the book may vary from the original edition.

Set in 16 pt. Plantin by Juanita Macdonald.

Printed in the United States on permanent paper.

Library of Congress Cataloging-in-Publication Data

Every woman has a story : many voices, many lessons, many lives :
   true tales / compiled by Daryl Ott Underhill.
      p.   cm.
   ISBN 0-7838-8753-1 (lg. print : hc : alk. paper)
   1. Women — United States — Social conditions Anecdotes.
   2. Women — United States Biography Anecdotes. 3. Women —
   United States — Conduct of life Anecdotes. I. Underhill, Daryl Ott.
   [HQ1421.E88 1999b]
   305.4´0973—dc21   99-38417

THIS BOOK IS DEDICATED TO YOU

Acknowledgments

This book honors the extraordinary individuals who have illuminated the passages with their true tales, leaving an indelible impression. To the awe-inspiring personalities who have shared their insightful encouragement, I express my gratitude.

I'm grateful for the love and support of my family and wonderful friends. I'd especially like to thank my beautiful mother, Mary Fithian, for her assistance throughout the process of this book project. Also, I am deeply touched by the support of my sister Lori Clark, and the exchange of thoughts and stories we share. Thanks to Barbara Fithian for her help and patience, Scott Fithian for his sense of humor, Greg Fithian for his vote of confidence, and my dad, William Fithian, for his positive attitude toward life.

I'd like to thank my agent, Jillian Manus, and my publisher, for believing in me and this book. I really appreciate the professional integrity and valuable suggestions offered by two very special women, my editors, Jamie Raab and Diana Baroni.

I especially would like to thank my son, Will Ott, for his humor, caring spirit, and perceptions of life and people. My first thoughts of doing this book were a result of a life passage we share. A special thanks to my husband, Michael Underhill, who creatively balances my life with love and understanding.

Chapters of Life

Motherhood

From One Generation to Another

Life's Lessons

A Time for Healing

The Emptying Nest

Follow Your Dream

Remembering with Love

Independent Woman

Simple Pleasures

Introduction

Every woman has a story, and it is through our stories we pass from one portal of life to another. The very essence of a woman's life is a compilation of her experiences.

Do you remember the small diaries that had a lock and key? Now they're called "journals." I often wonder what ever happened to mine. I used to hide it under my mattress so my little brothers and sister wouldn't find it and tease me mercilessly. Contained within the pages of this diary were my private thoughts. As a young girl this is where I figured life out, writing about my passages. On these pages, I learned to forgive my sister for snapping off the dancing ballerina on my musical jewelry box — even though it was an incident I provoked. This is where I forgave myself for accidentally sitting on my little brother's helicopter only moments after he found it under the Christmas tree. And this is where I examined the advice I'd given my other brother, when he was going to his first party. Tough challenges of life in those days. It's all relative; as we mature, so do our challenges.

Writing, and talking to other girls, enabled me to evaluate my life, decide where I fit, and discover my dreams, as I traveled through the years of my youth. Talking to others helped me to feel not so alone in my thoughts, and it is how I learned about life. No matter what the age, every woman has a story and, as evidenced in this book, most of the women began jotting down their feelings at very young ages, and still do. Some of the women in this book were robbed of their girlhoods, and their writing is what helped them survive. Communicating, in any form, can be an enlightening and therapeutic exercise.

When I put the call out for women's stories, I asked for stories straight from the heart. The message conveyed was more important than the writing style, because I wanted to feel what was being conveyed. I received over five hundred stories from women all over the world. Some were handwritten; some were from writers, others were not. I can honestly say that there was not one story that did not touch me. They were all from the heart. I cried, I laughed, I thought about people I knew, and I reflected upon my own experiences. I gained new insights, and I found I needed a little time between stories to digest, recover, and think. Reading the stories, you can almost hear these women's voices, and I empathized with all of them, regardless of the grammar, style, and other idiosyncrasies. I imagined these women talking and sharing their tears, laughter, and insight. The stories that are featured were difficult to select because every woman had a worthwhile tale.

Before you begin, I ask you to approach this book with more of your heart than your mind, and put your red pencils away. The true tales have been fine-tuned for easy reading; however, the many voices, many lessons, and many lives have been left unedited to perfection. I want you to look beyond the technical flaws of the writing and embrace their messages. Our lives aren't perfect, and then again, they aren't supposed to be. Accept the imperfect stories of life, and you will nourish your mind and exalt your spirits.

The topics vary, covering timeless and contemporary issues that women of all ages and backgrounds face along the path of life. I interviewed each woman and a profile follows her story. My credentials are simple: I am a woman, with viewpoints based on what I know and what I've learned. Like you, and the women in this book, I have formed opinions based on the events of life. We might not agree with one another, but I maintain we can still gain insight from sharing our stories and use the information as a guide to light our passages. Women prosper from woman-to-woman talk, and through the gift of exchange, we can enrich and rejuvenate our hearts and souls.

Daryl

Women
and
Friendship

The Circle of Decades

Cay Randall-May, Ph.D.

Circles fascinate me. Our lives are full of them, from a baby's teething ring to the rims of granny's reading glasses. The circles that have changed me most were formed by people holding hands. The "circle of decades" at my friend Carol's croning ceremony will always be in my memory, like a safety ring tied to the side of a boat. In case of near drowning, I'll toss it out and use it to stay afloat until the storm subsides.

It began as a gathering of women in the rosy amber twilight of a spring evening in Tucson. We were friends whose lives were about to inter-twine in a strong braid of shared experience. Our leader asked us to sum up the memories of each decade of our lives. "What was it like to be in your twenties?" I was glad I wasn't the first to speak, because it took a moment for me to recon-nect with that intense, fiery, burn-the-candle-at-three-ends woman/child of the 1960s who I had been. Sensuous and fanatically serious, I was mesmerized with dreams of impossible achieve-ment. Memories of graduate school in Berkeley crashed like breakers on my heart as I could al-most hear the distant refrain of "We shall over-come . . ." It was certainly interesting to have been in my twenties in that era, but I could also remember the skimp of the miniskirt and the size-five jeans that I slithered into like a snake shedding its skin in reverse. I felt relief when those of us no longer in our twenties were asked to take a step forward, tightening the circle.

"Now, share what it was like to be in your thirties," our leader prompted. My eyes closed. Sounds of birth cries, the primal embrace of a totally trusting swaddled infant, the smell of baby powder and diapers overwhelmed me. I had discovered the most difficult and rewarding job of all, motherhood, at the age of thirty. My thirties were a time of changed priorities, deflated party balloons, struggle with budgets, and plain hard work. Would I willingly return to that time of snowsuits and runny noses, putting the Christmas tree in the playpen to keep it from the toddlers? I don't think so, but I didn't want to step forward, either.

Because the next step was the forties, and those who had experienced this decade sighed with me. How could ten short years have held such highs and lows? I wished the twilight were a little deeper so no one could see the tears creeping down my cheeks, but other faces were also glistening. My story of ending a nineteen-year marriage and remarrying a man more attuned to my heart was not unique. Many others had found the forties to be a decade of major endings and beginnings. My hard-won career as a biologist, desperately precious to me at one time, had changed into a more spiritual and philosophical path. This decade, which began in gut-stabbing sorrow, ended in joy.

Another inward step, this time not so tentative, brought us to the fifties. Eyes began to sparkle again and I heard the giggles of those relieved to have once more survived their forties. We who were privileged to stand in the fifties decade shared newly explored interests, old talents polished like jewels, and we were finding our true path and power. As each woman shared her joyful enthusiasm for inner growth, I began to wonder what the next step would bring. What would women in their sixties share? Could that decade possibly be as good as the fifties, or was it the downward side of the mountain, as I had always been led to expect. I held back as the circle squeezed closer.

One by one, the members of the inner circle shared stories of personal freedom, new loves, the joys of grandchildren, travel and adventures, punctuated with smiles and glowing glances. All this enthusiasm caught my attention like a snow cone on a June afternoon. There was something worth knowing here. The women in this circle of decades were becoming more profoundly happy as they matured. A sliver of doubt wedged in my mind that maybe it was just something about the sixties decade that was so rewarding. Surely, the seventies would be different. My doubts didn't last long.

Our leader proudly stepped forward, the only

representative of the seventies, to become the heart of our circle. We raised her in our hearts like team members parading a triumphant star athlete. Her vigorous, wise-woman leadership spoke decibels louder than any words she could say. What I experienced that afternoon in the "circle of decades" helped me edit my life's script so that I look forward to the challenges and transitions ahead.

The ancient ceremony of croning was conducted when a woman stopped menstruating. It was an initiation into a "wise women's club," enabling the women to hold positions of power. Cay's story was based on a croning ceremony she attended. "It was a unique opportunity for us to review our lives. This moment of honest sharing gave me the priceless gift of a new vision, a hopeful pattern for aging." Cay is a professional intuitive consultant, she lectures on various topics related to creativity and intuitive development, and she teaches a course entitled "Intuitive Heart Discovery Process."

Letters to Friends

Jane Stebbins

I mailed 323 letters to friends last year.

And 437, the year before that.

I received four replies, not including the increasingly illegible notes from my grandfather and the token letter from my congressman.

I'd been putting this off, this spring cleaning, for about three years. And that day was the perfect day to do it: Outside, the clouds were pregnant with rain, inside, a fire cracked and popped in the woodstove.

With each name in my address book that was to be erased would go a history, a few more memories of the good times shared and the chances of ever getting the friendship back. I didn't want to let go of any of them, regardless how tenuous the hold.

I took a deep breath, flipped my pencil over, and cracked open the worn pages of the leather-bound book. A piece of paper fell to the floor, one of many with which the book was stuffed. It bore an address I wasn't sure at the time would reach permanent status in my book.

The name was familiar, as was the face; they all were. This one, from a high school chum with whom I was reunited at an impromptu party when I went home for Grandma's funeral, was crumpled up and tossed aside.

Melissa Anderson, with whom I'd shared numerous cups of coffee in college as we struggled through ornithology, was my next victim. A great writer while in college, her high-stress career on Wall Street long ago knocked me off her list of priorities.

Deb Bowie would be third. The scrawny woman with stringy hair and a shrill Massachusetts accent had pulled me out of more problems than I could count. Where she was anymore, I didn't know. I knew that at thirty-three, she had become a grandmother, having adopted her grandson as her own.

Gary and Rosemary. Cocaine, divorce, jail. Erased.

Hedwig Diehl. My other Grandma. She'd died last April; it was all I could do to erase her name from the top "Name/Address/City" line where her name had sat, in a child's block letters, for twenty-four years.

Juan Florence. Another high school buddy, ravaged by alcohol after the deaths of his parents.

The Filmores. His name got erased — death requires that. He was the minister who married us, atop a 10,350-foot mountain. He was eighty-three years old when we asked if he'd conduct the ceremony; that he would have to take a screeching ski lift to the summit didn't faze this man. "I'll be that much closer to heaven," he said.

24

Kristen Holland. The hardest one to erase, and one I shall never forget. I was engaged to her older brother for years before we finally called it quits. But I kept in touch with Kristen, even after she announced her homosexuality. She was disowned by her family, including the man I had once loved. I can still see her short white-blond hair whipping from side to side as she bounced all over the dance floor of our favorite bar. That woman never missed a moment of life.

The rain began to fall outside and the wind picked up.

The *I*'s, *J*'s, and *K*'s were left unscathed, but *L* was where it all fell apart.

Janet Loren. The name brought a smile to my face. We'd met on a Grateful Dead tour and traveled from California to Maine, Washington to Florida, dancing the dance that never ended to the music that never stopped. She's probably on a Phish tour, now that Jerry's gone, I thought. Sholyo Im Fi Zhami, Janet. Sholyo.

Albert Lowe. We went back to the fifth grade, when he sat across from me in Mr. Ash's class. He was the first boy — and Chinese (my mother would have died) — I felt I really loved. Eleven-year-old unrequited puppy love. The last time I saw him, we were drinking froufrou drinks and betting on the ponies.

Ann Long. She wouldn't remember me anymore, since she was struck by a car and suffered enough brain damage to keep her in a coma for months. She'd never be the same, but I'd kept her name in my book for all these years. Just in case. People come out of comas, I told myself.

Among those who survived the carnage of my eraser was Caroline Winters, my first best friend, who moved to Ireland when I was ten, and she twelve. I wrote her today, one of thirty-seven letters written while the rain pounded down outside. One last chance, for both of us.

I closed the book and tucked it away. It was a lot thinner for my efforts, a small pile of crumpled paper lay at my feet.

The names fell away in eraser crumbs, but they will be replaced by others in time.

But the memories, I hope, will linger on.

Jane is a newspaper editor and freelance magazine writer. She lives in Breckenridge, Colorado, with her husband, John, and seven-year-old daughter, Erin. When I asked her what prompted her story, she said, "I was writing letters and thinking how few people write back, and how sad it is that friendships fade away."

Webs

Sue Espinosa

I have several friends
we are all of an age
changing
   pausing
      rearranging
poised on a millennium edge
huddled together on a cosmic window ledge.

Among us — healers and crones
skeptic and dry bones
we live here and there
   each to her own lair
divided by zones
held together by phones.
we fling out hope
like colored strands of rope
and catching the skeins
   we eat jelly beans
while tying knots
   and sharing thoughts.
It is thus that we weave
wondrous webs with leaves
tiny seeds and great deeds
with little dreads
   and golden threads

with bits of magic
    and some things tragic
and in the weaving
    the giving and the receiving
we soothe our soul
connected and whole.

We are wives and mothers,
nurses, nuns, and daughters
    mud-covered
    star-studded
    blood-rivered
from large to small
goddesses all.
But separate us
one from the other
we eat
    we weep
        and then we sleep
burying our strength so far under
it becomes as powerful as lightningless thunder.
We boom and trill
    whine and shrill
casting about
    consumed by doubt
churning
    yearning
with wanton disregard
we discover the sacred
    now scarred.
The power once given in trust
vanquishes and eludes us.

It smashes and destroys
denuding our joys
and lost in leaden slumber
our heavy bodies lumber
ugly, incomplete
    our spirit deplete
we seek to find
    some rent in time
a fairy, a saint
    a new coat of paint
and then we recall
the web that relates us all.

And so we cast our dreams
in shimmering streams
    undiluted
    surefooted
    woman-rooted
we reconnect
in every aspect.

Sue is an independent-event and marketing consultant, mother of four, grandmother of two. She feels she has had the good fortune to meet and become friends with several remarkable women. "They are a source of wisdom and nourishment for me, as I am for them." Most of her friends are not in the same geographical area, and they rely on the telephone, writing, and occasional visits to nourish the friendship. Her poem was inspired by speaking with friends who were wrestling with the same issues, and realizing that she wasn't alone.

Coming Home

Jennifer Fales

My mother, my sister, and I are, at times, as different as the seasons. There are years between us, the many experiences of adulthood that we have not shared together, and other differing emotions and opinions to separate us. Some time ago, my mother developed lupus, which, although it is a grief commonly shared among the family, is her own private struggle. My sister is discovering the wild, wonderful world of teaching budding adolescents, which is an experience I can only briefly remember from the viewpoint of a former adolescent. As for myself, I have been selling auto parts for the past six years, meanwhile writing in every spare moment and hoping desperately for some golden opportunity to drop into my lap out of the cheery blue sky. You may have guessed by now that I'm the hopeless dreamer of the family, always busy watching life pass me by.

This past January, I visited my mother and sister, who now conveniently live about an hour apart, for a few days, and I learned something about myself in the process. There is a tiny little corner of me that has always been terrified of family. It has something to do with the powerful bond, the intimacy that is demanded. As a child, I was always afraid of being swallowed up into this great big entity and never being able to find myself again. I struggled hard to find a voice to separate myself, creating wonderful imaginary worlds. Even now, I find myself drawn into daydreams, like exotic quicksand. I hate to admit this, but I'm just not as fond of the real world as some people think I should be. However, on my visit, I rediscovered that my real-world family can be fantastic, and they might even help heal some old wounds if I let them.

There is something about my sister that automatically brings out the silliness in me. I had almost forgotten it until I saw that old familiar face, more like my own than any other. There are five years between us, but they don't make a bit of difference now. It's almost like being reunited with myself, because no thoughts expressed between us are incomprehensible, no jokes ever hang in the air like an albatross. For once, I never have to worry about feeling stupid for making some arbitrary comment. It is the equivalent of pure, creative freedom.

For some reason, I have always viewed Paula as the perfect, logical daughter. She was better at math, her organizational skills were existent as opposed to mine, and she always managed to come out on top. I cannot begin to tell you how happy I was to see her apartment. It was, of course, very tastefully decorated, much more so than the hodgepodge I call home, but it looked like someone really lived there. There were no plastic covers on the furniture. Dishes lay in the sink, books sat on the floor, and there were papers strewn across the dining room table. God had just handed me a present, complete with bows and wrapping paper. I could barely contain my excitement.

We talked about a lot of things, especially our dreams. Both of us want so much more out of life than we'll probably ever find. Our childhoods were more violent than most, and we've always wondered how we might have turned out under different circumstances. Still, the human soul is a funny thing. Hardships tend to make it blossom and increase its strength. I think we both believe it was worth it to have had the kind of life that we experienced because it made us the women we are today. Well maybe not *all* the experiences, but we could be so much less than what we have become.

Our mother is such an extraordinary woman. She has had a life riddled with hardships, but she never gives up. There are times when I've wanted to sit with her and ask her how she does it, what keeps her going, but I don't think she likes to dwell on it much. When my sister and I walked through the door, her face lit up. She was so happy to have her two girls together again. I think it helped her in some small way, and us, as well.

The last evening we spent together, we were all sitting on the couch, talking, and it occurred to me how much I had taken for granted. Our lives were all so fragile, so transitory. How often had I overlooked them over the years, these two women who were so very precious to me? Suddenly, I had been initiated into this sacred sisterhood. We were women, we were family, and, together, we were home.

Jennifer shares her home with her two dogs, four cats, and "a wonderful man." Reflecting on her relationship with her mother and sister, she became aware of the strong connection they shared as women, and the significance of their friendship. "As I grow older and wiser, I am fortunate enough to realize how dear and precious family truly is."

The Day After
Parents' Night

Gail M. Hicks

I wore something cute and perky to the fourth-grade parents' night because I wanted to look good, even if I didn't feel that way. All schools make me feel as shy and insecure as when I myself was attending; but most especially does the elementary school that my youngest attends. At the middle school, all the parents are older than me, and I can relax in the knowledge that my hips are a little slimmer than most and my breasts a bit higher. But for the fourth-grade parents' night, I had to wear my cutest little red print mini and my sleeveless chambray weskit, high-heeled slings with no hose, and my biggest silver hoop earrings. I looked good, and, for a while, I was glad I had taken the effort.

I was the first to arrive, even before the teacher, because I am chronically early for everything. "Mrs. Straight, it's so nice to see you," said Mrs. Turly as she unlocked the classroom door. "Just find Erica's name tag, and you can sit at her desk." Parents began to fill the room, and, attempting to be anonymous, I retreated gratefully behind my cute, if binding, outfit. I am sure I was smiling my friendliest smile at everyone who caught my vacant gaze, when, suddenly, I found myself smiling up into a very familiar face. It was Tina Blanding, the cheerleader. For a very long moment, I was terrified, as of old, but when she did not recognize me, I thought, with no small amount of relief, that perhaps I was mistaken. But no, I couldn't be. She was fat and dressed frumpily in an oversized Hawaiian-print camp shirt and khaki pleated shorts, but there was no mistaking that pretty face. And then I remembered how very cute I looked, and the thought crossed my mind that perhaps I could approach the heretofore unapproachable Tina. After all, I thought, we are all adults, and I look so much better than her, she wouldn't have the nerve to snub me.

"Hi, I think I know you," I said. A faint glimmer of recognition showed on her face. "Are you Tina Blanding?"

"Carver High, right?" she replied.

"Yea, and actually, Washington Elementary, too."

"That's right." She smiled. "I thought I recognized you. I'm Tina Rayford now, but, I'm sorry, I don't remember your name."

"Cheryl Straight. Well, used to be Mc-Dunough."

"That's right, I do remember you," she said, in a way that made me wonder whether or not I should be happy about that.

Just at that moment, Mrs. Turly began to

speak, and we parents took our places at the desks of our respective children. I had done well, I thought. Well enough that I could relax a little and, yes, even be happy that Tina had remembered me, for whatever reason. Perhaps I had finally achieved a level of social status equal to the great Tina Blanding: cheerleader, socialite, popular person.

My feelings of equality, however, were short-lived, for, when I attempted to speak with Tina at the end of the evening, she seemed bothered by the whole affair. She was polite, but then quickly excused herself when I started to suggest that we and our daughters might get together sometime. She very hurriedly said good-bye to Mrs. Turly and left the room. Again, I had been snubbed. How silly of me to think that she and I could be friends. I am a nobody, and she is a somebody, and never the twain shall go shopping together.

I did not think of Tina again until the following spring. I was grateful to my daughter for not befriending Tina's, for this way, I could easily assist Tina in avoiding me altogether — and we had not so much as crossed paths for the past seven months. I kept myself safe and did not place my feelings where their care would not be certain.

But feelings are uncertain and safety illusive. And shortly before school's end, a note came home. There had been a death: a parent of one of the students in my fourth grader's class. After a long struggle with breast cancer, the note said,

36

Mrs. Tina Rayford was dead. The school psychologist would be speaking in each of the three classes affected to guide the children through the grieving process. "Please call the appropriate number for questions or help," it said: something I will always wish I had done the day after parents' night.

Gail believes learning and growing are forever and ongoing, painful and humorous, humiliating and uplifting. "Growing up is hard to do, and just when you think you're finished, you find yourself in need of more growth." She is the single mother of three "wonderful (most of the time) children." She is currently working toward her B.A. in women's studies.

Year
by
Year

I'm Thirty — And That's Okay

Pattie Johnson

I knew it was morning without opening my eyes. Sunlight flooded the bedroom and crept inside my tightly closed lids, forbidding further sleep. I stretched out my right leg, then my left, pointing my toes to awaken the slumbering muscles. It was amazing! I still had feeling in my limbs. I pulled my arms above my head and interlocked the fingers to stretch again. It was that same tingling feeling that I had experienced in my legs; the feeling of muscles being pulled from their restful bliss. They felt alive. I felt alive. Guess what? There is life after thirty. My first complete day of thirty-something had started okay, so I decided to venture forth and see what else the world had to offer a three-decade-old lady. I opened the refrigerator door in search of breakfast. Hmm, brown lettuce and green bread. Then I spied *it!* Chocolate cake left over from last night's party. Mother would never approve! But hey, Mother wasn't in my kitchen right now. I was thirty years old, and if I wanted to eat chocolate cake for breakfast, I could. It was my right of passage.

Next, I decided to put this tridecade body to the test. I pulled my bike down from its rack and started for the great outdoors. As an afterthought, I grabbed my cycling helmet. They say that the gray matter starts to disappear after the age of thirty. I figured that at this age, I needed all the help I could get.

The nature trail was busy that morning. There was the usual assortment of "perfect tens" — you know, the ones with shares in the Spandex corporation. I often looked at those women with envy, their lean, taut bodies straight from the magazine glossies. But today, they looked different.

Maybe it was the sunshine, maybe the thirtyish outlook that was starting to grow on me — or maybe it was the chocolate cake. I didn't know. What I did know was that if they were tens and I was thirty, I was three times better than them. Of course, I knew by looking at their bodies that, in fact, they were in better shape than I was, but for the first time, it didn't matter. Some people had better bodies than me and some people had worse. That was okay.

Looking back at my first year of thirty-something, I learned that there is life after thirty, and if you embrace what it teaches you, it's even better than life before that magical number. I learned that I will never have a "perfect ten" body. I looked at the body I had, accepted it, exercised regularly, and consumed lots of fruits and vegetables. It responded appropriately, but it will never grace the pages of a fitness magazine. But that's okay — signing autographs for adoring fans is far too time consuming for someone like me.

I learned that I don't have to conform to, or fulfill society's or anyone else's expectations. I do things now that I wouldn't have five or six years ago. Am I still anxious when I test new ground? Sure I am. But I think to myself, When I am ninety-five, will I look back at my life and have regrets? The thought that I could possibly respond yes frightens me even more than experiencing the unknown. It's okay to be unsure of the future. Feed off your hesitancy and the world will offer you many rewards. I often wish that I could bottle the knowledge that I gained upon turning thirty. I would sell it to teenagers, making the unsure agony of adolescence more bearable. It would teach them that the "perfect ten" body is not worth starving yourself or dying for. It would teach them that there is only one person that they have to measure up to and that is him- or herself.

But then I think, wait a minute. It is the culmination of my teenage experiences combined with those of my twenties that has blessed me with the insight that I now have. It took thirty years of learning, but on my thirtieth birthday, I was granted the ultimate knowledge; I'm not perfect, but neither is the rest of the world . . . and that's okay.

Pattie's story was based on a conversation with a friend who was also approaching a thirtieth birthday with hesitation. "We found that the acceptance and serenity that followed was definitely worth the wait. In your twenties, you are unstable and continually making changes to find your place. In your thirties, you've found your groove, and it is comfortable. It fits you, although it may not be where you wanted to be (you wanted to be thinner, richer, etc.). You are comfortable enough to try new things and make changes, knowing fully that if things don't work out, your groove is still there, waiting for you like an old friend." Pattie finds courage to try new things, and when changes are necessary, the inner peace will help her through.

Little Fairies of Youth

Leslie Hudgins

The line curled down the sidewalk. I parked my minivan and propelled myself past the loiterers. I was first at the end of the line. It crept up six inches. Progress already. My stomach growled. I was missing my scheduled consumption of food. I reminded myself this was the most convenient procedure for summer school registration. My son didn't drive because his grades were deficient enough to warrant a session in summer school. This was one of the times I wished we'd relented about "the rules." The rules were supposed to build character. He was consorting with his friends and I was standing in a long line. I wondered how his character was feeling today.

The sun was doing a vicious dance on the back of my neck. My stomach whimpered. Oblivious teenagers wandered to the line's end. The boy in front of me was chaperoned by his mother, a matron with a large patent-leather purse and sensible shoes. He was a nice clean-cut kid in a sea of oddities. He didn't even look like a summer school applicant, with his evenly trimmed hair and brand new T-shirt. I knew it was a brand-new shirt because there was one of those clear sticky labels that read X-TRA LARGE, X-TRA

LARGE, X-TRA LARGE on his back. It was directly in my line of vision. I wanted to peel it away and present it to him in a gesture of goodwill, but I refrained. His mother didn't appear to be enjoying the experience. Her purse looked as if it might contain something heavy.

We were moving. The young man in front of "Mr. X-tra Large" was dressed entirely in black. I began to sweat in sympathy. Dirty blond hair hung in a tangled mane from underneath a black hat, summer school material for several years. He probably thought he was ultracool. I waited in anticipation to get a glimpse of this rock star. He rotated his head, checking if anyone was observing. His face was a topographical map of acne; peaks and valleys decorated his profile.

He was just a gaunt kid, similar to "Mr. X-tra Large." Without his disguise, he would've fallen victim to a horde of tough guys anxious to verify their manhood. Instead of being victimized, he transformed himself into Zorro. He became a symbol of youth's uniqueness, establishing himself an acceptable place in their odd society. What a clever camouflage: The swan was really just an ugly duckling.

Little tributaries of sweat were meandering down my spine. Teenage girls assembled, laughing, clucking, various shades of man-made red hair bobbing. Some sat casually on the smoldering sidewalk curbs, bare flesh against concrete. I could feel the substantial heat oozing through the soles of my shoes. *Were they oblivious to everything?* My own son was so much like the other foreigners — unresponsive, uncommunicative. He was a teenage zombie, glazed eyes, arms extended, searching for money or sustenance. Although he appeared alien to me, he was continually surrounded by a herd of teenagers who found his wit razor-sharp, and they were drawn to him like disciples, moths to a flame.

My stomach howled. I squashed forward so I could secure a wisp of the seeping air conditioning. I stared with lust at the shaded doorway. . . . *Then the goddess surfaced.* There was nothing unusual about her appearance. She looked like a thousand girls, but she altered my consciousness in the seconds it took her to pass by. Trailing her was an aura so delicious, I forgot about the sweat, heat, and the check I was about to write. Her hair was damp, drying in the sunlight, moist curls tickling her neck. Her legs were firm and brown underneath cutoff jeans. Her sandaled feet paraded past, adorned with tiny pink toenails. I detected herbal shampoo in her hair, the starchiness in her crisp shirt . . . her youth. I transcended to a time and place I had forgotten existed.

In her wake, she left behind a taste of being young again. I rolled it around in my mind, savoring its flavor, salivating at its scent. I remembered being pure and new, ecstatic about being alive. I ached for her opportunities and yearned for her experiences. I could faintly taste her vitality, and I became an old vampire, touching her pulse. I wanted a first kiss, a last dance, a bridge to cross. She drifted among the parked cars and her apparition faded as I struggled to cling on for a few seconds longer.

I am awake. I am almost forty.

I did my motherly duty and wrote the check that would ensure my son's chance to conquer the world. Little fairies of youth danced around my head. I smiled at Zorro on my way to the car.

Leslie is married with two children, and has had several of her poems published. Her thoughts on growing older and a personal experience provoked her story: "I have always enjoyed writing and documenting my thoughts. I am finally forty. . . . It's not as bad as I had anticipated."

Déjà Vu

Wanda Parker

Salty sea air, mingled with the nearby paper factory, reeked of an egg salad sandwich forgotten in your lunch sack. The slow screech of the patched screened door alerted me to their entry. In they strolled, sand-crusted bare feet leaving dusty patchwork patterns on the aged oak floors. The twinkle of innocent laughter between young friends on a sizzling summer's day floated beneath the whirling ceiling fan.

With fading eyesight, I assessed them from the sundry section. One, pretty with the promise of blossoming beauty, was wearing oversized shorts and a teensy tight blouse in some unearthly color that had died from numerous washings. A mass of wiry curls covered her head like a helmet of Slinkys. Her chubby legs, buttery-fat and adolescent-awkward, were covered in sticker scratches — each mark a story of some insignificant happening, fading as quickly as the innocence of youth.

The other captured my attention. Tall, with flaming red hair that the sun's rays seemed to set on fire, she glided with effortless elegance, her arms swinging in graceful movements. Her limbs, moving feather-light, caressed the craggy floor as she drifted through my store. Sagging straps supported the dress that once boasted cheery flowers but was now wilted and faded from uncountable scrubbings and sun. On her dress, bulging pockets were filled with shells and sand, gifts from secret places of the sea that are given up each night with the tide. Each a prized possession to be taken home and placed in a special container that would eventually migrate into the dark recesses of an unused closet.

They sauntered lazily through the vegetable section. My ears strained to hear the unique language of best friends, spoken with a minimum of words and expression. Their weightless voices blended with the consistent hum of the ancient freezer that ceases to be noticed unless it stops running. Approaching the freezer with the anticipation of greeting an old chum, a gust of frigid air pelted them unrepentantly on their sticky, sunburned faces as they peered inside the chest of frozen treasures. Stacked in neat rows lay Brown Cows, Popsicles, orange Push-ups, and Mayfield Neapolitan cups.

Following much animated discussion, they selected my favorite, a cherry Popsicle, protected by paper coated in freezer frost. They paid for their treat, and my fading eyes followed them as they departed, leaving behind a powerful essence of déjà vu, containing girl smells reminiscent of my childhood. Suntan oil, summer sweat, and the fading scent of Evening in Paris bathed me in soothing waters of the past and quenched my thirst for the sweet flavor of life.

As the door slammed shut, a wad of tissue, devised to deny pesky insects free admission into the store, fell out of the torn screened door. Plopping down on the sandy, sagging front steps of the kudzu-covered store, the tall one methodically peeled the paper away from the prize inside. She secured the shiny Popsicle carefully between two hands with the expertise of a surgeon making the first incision. She cut it quickly and cleanly into two even pieces of frozen ruby red juice on a stick and shared half with her friend. Silence fed the moment as they relished and paid homage to the treat. Darting tongues lightly kissed the icy-cold glistening confection as the summer's heat and humidity inherited its share of the Popsicle. The frosty treat began to melt and drip a lengthening trail of bright red down their chins and arm. The sandy earth savored the sticky sweetness as they bent forward between their legs to enjoy the last dribbles of sugary nectar. The Popsicle finished, they discarded the cherry-stained wooden stick. The only remaining evidence were their dyed red tongues and lips.

Their heads bent together in a shared secret, they chuckled, stood, and stretched their bodies, catlike, in contentment. The long-legged one, posed in the practiced posture of a dancer, attended to the sand that clung to her dress and the back of her legs, with as much care and concern as an old widow readying herself for an evening out with a gentleman friend. The other, oblivious to her sand-covered shorts, squirmed her brown feet in the cool white sand. Satisfied, the tall one gracefully extended her hand to her friend, and off they ran toward the beach.

Patting my graying hair, which years ago was so teased and taunted that it resembled a fiery bonfire, my bent body awakened into the fifth position of ballet. Scrunching my tangled toes, I recalled the tight fit of my pink toe shoes.

As the girls disappeared into the misty vapor of the sultry summer's day, a smile escaped my dry, wrinkled face as my heart embraced the shadow of resurrected memories, and our spirits touched across an abyss of time.

Wanda is a wife and mother of four "by design," and a writer by heart. She is presently a student pursuing a degree in women's psychology. After returning to college at the age of forty-six, she rediscovered her love of writing. She boasts, "I have embarked on a new journey . . . my own rites of passage!" Reinforced with her youthful frame of mind, she is working on a collection of fiction that gives voice to women and their passages.

The Great Omelet Caper

Corey Seemiller

It's only about a month before my eighteenth birthday, but for some reason I don't feel seventeen. The restaurant is pretty cold, and I'm sitting here alone. Two months ago, I never could have gone anywhere alone. It would not have been the cool thing to do. But I'm different now. For the first time in my life, I feel mature. I don't have to blast the stereo in my car to enjoy the music, or be obnoxious to my teachers in school. I just look back and realize that I've moved on from that.

I must admit, the strangest part about growing up is that I'm beginning to act grown-up. When I was younger, I remember my parents always ordering omelets when we went out to breakfast. It was never even a choice for me to order something other than the syrupy pancake special. It was as though ordering an omelet was a sign of being an adult.

What happened to when we were younger, when the only plan we had in the world was playing with the neighbors? I remember coming home from school, throwing my books by the front door, and running out to play until I collapsed with exhaustion. My mom would go out to the yard and bring me in for a macaroni and cheese and hot dog dinner. We would eat on snack trays in the family room while my parents watched their favorite TV shows. I watched right along with them, not knowing or caring who the characters were. I would then get tucked into bed to prepare for the next exciting day. What a life! My only worries then were who was on whose team for kickball at recess and whether or not my class was going to have a substitute teacher that day.

I think about whether or not I would go back to third grade if I had the chance. Life then was easy. Life now is confusing. Growing up is confusing. But I would never change it for the world. I'm ready to go full force into adulthood, and I realize that in ten years I'll probably look back to when I was seventeen and see myself as a child. It's all part of growing up.

I better find the waitress and order, because I'm tired and I want to get home and go to sleep for work tomorrow. Here she comes. "Yes, I would like a cup of coffee and the Belgian waffle with the whipped-cream smiley face."

As Corey, now an adult with a master of education degree, was sorting through old papers, she found this story, which she had written when she was seventeen.

What Scares Me Most...

Jessica Lynn Muery

What scares me most in life is death. I'm an atheist, so I probably fear death more than someone who faithfully believes that they will transcend into a better world. I believe that if I don't do it in this lifetime, that's it — no second chances! It's not the thought of no longer existing that scares me; it's the fear of dying before I experience all of the finer benefits that mortal life has to offer and before I become cognizant of the true meaning of my time here.

I fear the obvious . . . like no longer experiencing my great-grandchildren giggle and play, the magic of a warm Hawaiian breeze, the beauty of an Arizona sunset, baseball games at Wrigley Field, and ice cream in Central Park. Yet this exemplifies only a small portion of my fear. What I fear most are the thoughts that will be going through my mind moments before death. More specifically, will I be impressed with who I was and what I represented throughout my life? Will I die wise with self-respect, or will I die calloused with regret? As I look into a mirror when I'm facing the gates of death, will laugh lines boldly frame my sparkling, blissful eyes, or will I stare into a cold and empty face? Will I see strength, honesty, adventure, wit, loyalty, ambition, confidence, imagination, courage, and integrity, or will I just not care?

Did I take the time to find beauty in objects and people? Did I love without fear of rejection? How many times did I change for the better? Did I take my intelligence to its full potential? Was I a role model for someone who desperately needed one? Did I work hard? Did I always find time for those who needed me most? Are my children proud that I was their mother? Did I treat others as I hoped they would treat me? Did I fight for worthy causes? Did I take every precious moment of life and use it to its full potential, or did I let it slip away like it meant nothing?

I'd much rather die of exhaustion than of boredom. Dying apathetic and bored is the very root of my fear. Yet as I lie in my bed all day long, afraid that I'll fail to meet all the expectations I've set for myself, I find that today is just one more day that I'll spend feeling like I just don't care.

Jessica graduated from college in 1993, a young woman with wise insights. "I wrote this story after losing a teaching job. Expressing my thoughts on paper has always helped me put in perspective what was really important in my life." Soon after, she took another teaching position, where she learned computer skills. Her acquired computer skills led her to a career change, and she has realized the world is full of challenges that can lead to great opportunities.

Men
and
Love

Making It

Carol E. Braff

Dressed in a white-and-lavender sundress and white flat shoes, I stood beside my father in the chapel foyer. Ecstatic about being married, I was terrified of walking without my leg brace or cane.

When the music started, I hesitantly moved forward. I carried a floral bouquet in my unfeeling left hand while I clung firmly to my dad's arm with my right. The aisle looked five miles long and I wasn't sure I could make it to the altar. When I saw David smile at me from the altar, my courage was rejuvenated.

When we became engaged, David and I had no inkling our wedding plans would soon be drastically altered or that my life would be indelibly changed. Active and athletic at thirty-two, I began to experience some unusual symptoms. I felt a strange sensation of heaviness in my head when in a bending head-down position during Jazzercise. I also had severe headaches that I offhandedly attributed to a chronic sinus condition. Then my right eye began to bulge. When my right temple began to distend, I knew it was time to see my doctor.

After extensive medical tests, his diagnosis was arteriovenous malformation (AVM), a congenital birth defect of the brain. As the malformation grows, it causes the veins to enlarge and the arteries to bleed. The malformation is usually not detectable at birth and, as in my case, may not manifest symptoms for many years.

My doctor referred me to a specialist in neurosurgery. This specialist is a world-renowned authority on AVM. A kindly man with a golden aura, he instantly intrigued me. When we shook hands, I felt deeply touched by him. When we made our first eye contact, I trusted him.

The doctor explained the AVM: "When you were one inch long in your mother's womb, you had it," he told me. "The only treatment is surgical removal." When he said that he would remove thousands of defective veins and arteries from my brain, it took a while for me to comprehend. Without treatment, he explained, there was greater than a 50 percent chance I would suffer disability from a stroke. He indicated there was an excellent chance for full recovery, a 10 to 20 percent chance of partial sensory deprivation, and a 1 percent chance of dying. It was also possible I would require more than one surgery. I reluctantly accepted his diagnosis and, spurred by my prospects for a full recovery, agreed to the surgery.

The operation lasted ten hours, but the doctor still could not fully appraise the extent of the malformation. I would definitely need a second surgery and maybe more. Meanwhile, I had an incision scar that began at my right temple, curved about three inches above the ear, and ended at the base of my skull.

It eventually took six operations to completely remove the AVM. After the sixth and final surgery, I felt an enormous sense of relief. Finally, David and I could plan our wedding. The dream was really going to come true. I was immensely thankful to the man who, with his skilled hands, had made me well again, had crafted new life into my ailing being.

Eight hours later, I experienced complications from blood clots in the small vessels that extend into the brain tissue. Emergency surgery was performed, and when I woke up, I was completely paralyzed on my left side.

Confined to a wheelchair and forced to wear a leg brace, I began an intensive program of physical therapy. Through sheer willpower, I gradually began to regain strength. After three months in the wheelchair, I graduated to a walker. To use the walker, I stabilized my left side with the leg brace and moved it forward with my right arm. I was still without sensation over most of my left side. I knew my recovery would be long and arduous, but I was determined to overcome my affliction regardless of what physical, mental, and spiritual effort it took.

Now I was walking, without my leg brace or cane, down the chapel aisle to marry David. I was frightened that I would drop the flowers that my left hand could not feel, or, even worse, stumble and fall. When I saw David waiting for me, I felt an emotional rush of love for the man who had stayed with me through the turmoil and disheartenment of my adversity.

Finally, I made it to the altar and, holding David's hand, celebrated in triumph as the minister pronounced us man and wife.

Carol's husband recently surprised her with a renewal of their wedding vows. He reinvented the same wedding, with the same people and in the same place, to celebrate their twelfth anniversary. "He's so romantic, and I was surprised!" She is the mother of two boys and has had years of struggle juxtaposed with years of happiness.

Neurologically challenged, she says she "retrained my brain to walk, and move." She has strength, and full use of her body, but little sensation on her left side. She continues physical therapy and attends a Jazzercise class three times a week. "I am determined to overcome my disability."

There's Always Sunshine

Stephanie Morneau

It's funny how on my darkest days it's hard to find the sun. A few months ago, a man I loved very much told me there was no longer room in his life for me. Needless to say, my heart was broken. I was very sad about the loss of my lover, and, more importantly, a best friend. I didn't know I was about to embark on an amazing journey.

I began to question why this had happened, and tried to make sense of it all. The conclusion I came to was that life created this change so I could grow spiritually. In coming to this conclusion, I realized that I had another choice — that of avoidance. Although it seemed attractive at first, I knew the temporary comfort wasn't worth the price I would have to pay. It would have been an expensive price of greater pain and an inability to grow emotionally. Therefore, I chose the journey of growth.

This journey of growth I am encountering has not exactly been comfortable. It has been full of pain, sorrow, tears, and a whole lot of self-examination. Through this discomfort, I've discovered things in myself that make it all worthwhile. I think I heard it best summed up on one of those afternoon talk shows: "We cannot become what we need to be by remaining what we are."

Now I'm learning to embrace the changes in my life. More times than not, what seems like a bad change will open a whole new door of wonderful experiences and opportunities. We must keep in mind that past experiences will actually have positive effects if we let them. As we grow with the emotional challenges life brings us, blessings begin to fall like rain. Don't forget on those cloudy days that the sun still shines behind them. Before we know it, they'll start to clear and rainbows will again appear in our lives.

Stephanie's story reflects a turning point in her life. "I realized I had discovered new things about myself, and people, and I decided to seize the opportunity to expand my spirit and release the heartache." Understanding why he broke off the relationship, she truly felt sad for this man. Above all else, as she was sorting through her pain, she was thankful to him. "I realized I was worthy of and wanted a much deeper, equal relationship."

Dear You

Lori Johnson

There was a time when our lives were as one. We felt there was nothing we couldn't overcome as long as we were together. I gave you my heart, my mind, my body, and my soul. My faith and belief in you was endless and unnerving. We grew from our similarities and learned from our differences.

Spending time together was never a chore. We were each other's first priorities, but we had enough love and happiness to share with those around us. Even now, I can remember the touch of your lips on our first kiss, so tender, so nervous. And the feeling I had when I lay in bed that night, heart pounding, thinking of the next time we'd be together.

Your eyes would light up when you looked at me. My heart would jump when you said my name. I was never so sure of anything before. My world was centered by you. You were the only thing I knew I could always depend on. It was one of the few things I thought I never had to question. I felt blessed having you in my life.

I don't know what happened. I can torture myself for the rest of my life and never fully understand. The light in your eyes dimmed. And sometimes when you said my name, I would cringe. I fought to get back to where we were before, to the love I knew was still there . . . but all we ended up doing was pushing each other away. Every day there seemed to be a new brick in the wall that was being built between us. And as fast as I could knock them down, another would appear. I grew tired.

What I once thought was us becoming comfortable became distance, then resentment.

Now our one soul has become two again. My heart is filled with bitter anger, and as much as I want to, I seem incapable of hating you completely. Just the person you've become, not the person I fell in love with.

I've forced myself to sleep in the middle of the bed so I don't reach out for you. I got rid of all the gifts you gave me . . . all the pictures of us smiling together. When I come home, there's a different type of silence now — one that's comforting, not filled with tension. I don't think I miss you anymore, just the idea of you. A part of me will always love you, but not be in love with you.

You haven't broken me; I will survive this. I know that because I was able to love in the past, I'm capable of that again. One day I will smile again.

Lori was married on her twenty-second birthday and was separated three years later. Now twenty-seven, she lives in Ontario, Canada. She has survived — and is smiling once again.

Fall into Spring

Karen DeLuca Katchmeric

She had always loved the Fall; her birthday. The cooler weather, colorful falling leaves, Sunday drives through vivid scenic mountains, and chestnut hunting, when she was younger. Crisp, brisk mornings filled with blinding sunlight; the sound of chirping crickets and the breathtaking early sunsets. But this year was different. For the first time in a long time, she was alone.

He had walked out in the Spring — May, to be exact. In the middle of Spring cleaning, he decided that he wanted to be sprung. After fifteen years of marriage, he was going to turn forty soon and had to find himself. So he just left, left behind his messes in every corner of the house for her to clean up. Messes that she had never understood, but tolerated, because of her love for him. And she was paralyzed, all summer kept hoping that he would come back to her, to his piles of meaningless stuff, to finally help her clean it all up. But he never did. And now it was Fall. And she had to do something.

The cooler weather and turning leaves beckoned her, but so did the messy house. So she opened the windows and doors to let the Fall in as she cleaned. And pretty soon all the piles of stuff were outside and the garbage collectors picked them up and they were gone. And then he wanted to come home. And she said no.

She had finally done her Spring cleaning in the Fall, and had been sprung into a new life, in her favorite time of year. And she didn't have to leave to find out who she was. She had always known, and was looking forward to the Spring. It was a true birthday. Her life was no longer a mess.

Karen, in her early forties, is an attorney. She became disabled in 1992 with CFIDS fibromyalgia after taking Synarel for recurrent endometriosis. She was not properly diagnosed until 1995, and is currently improving with a combination of nutritional alternatives. No longer bedridden, she has become a home-based writer, which allows her to accommodate her still-somewhat-severe illness. Karen's marriage was stressed by the experience, and her husband left her in the spring of 1996, providing the inspiration for her story. She remains ever optimistic that her physical condition will continue to improve and that someday she may again practice law.

Falling in Love — Again

Linda Dietrick

You want to trust. You want to be in another relationship, but you're afraid. You've been hurt; you've been disappointed. You have trusted and ended up abused, sometimes even physically. Do you dare ever to trust again?

This is where I found myself at the age of forty-five. I was falling in love and I was falling apart because of it. Russ was everything that I wanted, but could I trust him with my heart?

Should I go further with this relationship? Should I get out of it while I could? Questions like this were causing me so much stress, I went to see a counselor. She taught me how to have confidence, to be able to see myself as a woman deserving of love and that I could try again.

"Are you happy with him?" she asked me.

"Well, of course," I answered, not even thinking about it.

"Then don't let fear stand between you and love, honey. Go for happiness."

It was true: Russ and I were happy. Our relationship was positive and free of the abuse of my previous relationships. Russ was a builder, instead of someone who tore down. So we became engaged and moved in together.

Russ had been hurt in the past, so we made a project out of trust. He encouraged me, did and said things to give me confidence, and was gentle with my feelings. I did the same for him. We did fight, but we set limits on it. We cried and apologized. He taught me, and I taught him. We talked, we learned, and we studied non-threatening ways we could work out our problems. We became like a rosebush in the spring, and we blossomed. Trust in love began to grow and flourish in the atmosphere that we were creating. Our friends and family would comment on how happy we were. They didn't realize how much work, love, and growth we poured on our rosebush. We weren't without problems, but we worked to find the solutions.

After three years, we decided we were strong enough for the big step — marriage. That was high anxiety! It brought back frightening memories for me of my first husband. For Russ, it meant commitment. We had to talk it out. The night before the wedding, we had such tension that we bruised each other in our sleep, tossing and turning.

We were so glad we did it, though. We had been married for five joyous months when Russ died suddenly. I had lost my best friend. Now I am so glad I chose happiness. I am glad I allowed myself to let love grow to its conclusion. The beauty it added to my life was well worth it. The love and confidence gleaned from our love not only left me with sweet memories but has empowered me to go after long-lost dreams. It took everything that I had to fight the fear I had and allow myself to love again, but I have come to believe that the beauty of life is given to the ones who overcome fear.

"I wrote this story because I believe it takes courage to get what you want in life, and to get past the hurts. I've had to do this so often in my life." Linda is now in her early fifties and is attending college where she studies naturopathy and counseling. Linda is not alone and finds solace with her two children, a stepdaughter, and two grandchildren.

A Shining Light

Nancy Gilpatrick

"I don't have any patients like you," said the doctor. I felt plugged into an electrical socket, my insides buzzing loudly. This wasn't the first time I'd heard what an unusual case I was medically. It was just that every time I heard it, I was shocked all over again.

I remember vividly the first time: sitting on the exam table in the surgeon's office. I casually asked, "Well, ah . . . did you get the bone-scan results?"

She said, "I was hoping you wouldn't ask. And yes, I did. The bone-scan is positive. There are several hot spots on your skeleton."

The room receded from my consciousness as I began to cry. I looked around the room, to the two people who I trusted implicitly: the surgeon and my partner, Terry. The surgeon had taken me through the past couple of weeks with firm guidance and she stood with her hand on my knee as I cried. I couldn't take in the information. Terry stood with his arms around me, reminding me with his warmth of his love for me. When we arrived at the office that afternoon, I'd noticed the usually warm, friendly staff seemed awkward with me — less eye contact and less joking. Even though I'd had the hip pain for several months, I hadn't allowed myself to consider the possibility of cancer. These things happened to other people.

In the days and weeks following my first visit to the surgeon, each appointment with the doctors brought more grim news. First, the breast cancer itself; the pathology report after surgery showed cancer in the lymph nodes. Followed by pictures of bone metastases in my hip and pelvis. Later, more news about bone fragility. Radiation was done, but there was no change. Again, promises of pain reduction via chemotherapy. No less pain after two rounds of drug therapy. Then, new films showed progression of the disease to my skull, thoracic spine, and across the pelvis to the right hip.

I began to despair. I had not wanted to believe this was a life-threatening disease. Yet, there was no reduction in cancer cells in my body, only more being produced. No lessening in bone pain, only more disability, more instability of the bones that held my body upright, making walking more difficult.

In the midst of my despair was a shining light, Terry and our relationship. We had an on-again, off-again relationship, with our passion and connection marred only by our individual ambivalence. One day in the middle of receiving this grim news, he called from work and said, "I think we need to talk about me moving in with you, to help you through these treatments." I was stunned. I felt a flood of joy run through my body. Here I was in the midst of a huge crisis and this man, Terry, was telling me he loved me and wanted to help me, to live with me, to share the roller-coaster ride.

We talked about living together. It was based on the idea of impermanence. Terry would move in for three to four months while I did a clinical trial involving four cycles of high-dose chemotherapy, each followed by a stem-cell transplant. First, he thought he'd just move over some clothes and his computer so he could write. Then he decided he'd bring his water bed. Once the water bed was moved and set up, he said he thought he'd rent his condominium. With enormous pleasure, I watched his process of allowing himself to get further involved with me.

Our relationship is filled with love and contentment, juxtaposed with pain and moments of despair. We've lain in bed and watched hummingbirds out our back door. We've read magazine after magazine at doctor appointments we thought would never end. He's held my head as I've vomited time after time. He's wheeled me through the hospital while we laughed at some private joke of ours. Trips out of town remind us life goes on. At a bed-and-breakfast, we watched piñon jays chase Cassin's finches off the feeder. Another trip south brought us to red rock country, arches, and desert sunsets. Mexico was our grandest adventure. Me with the walker at the border as Terry maneuvered the wheelchair and our bags onto the bus. At the beach, we watched brown pelicans fishing and Caspian terns diving.

I look for meaning in the breast cancer and its companion, despair. I want there to be gifts, not burdens. Our adventures remind me to live in the moment, with the wonder of having found a best friend, companion, lover, and life mate.

Terry and Nancy married shortly after he moved in with her and her children. She said they shared similar passions. "I have found my dream mate and I'm so very happy. Having lived a full life and experienced a hardship or two, I now know I need to discover the gifts in what's before me, in order not to get stuck in depression and despair."

I learned from Terry that Nancy passed away in December 1997 as a result of breast cancer. Her inspirational attitude, courage, and love for Terry will live on through her story. When we last spoke she told me, "A lifelong dream of mine has been to be a published writer. That dream is about to come true."

Lord Help the Sister

Sandi Boritz Berger

The day my best friend, Rona Wasserberg ("best dancer"), asked the love of my life, Jeffrey ("tepid in tennis"), to the annual Sadie Hawkins dance was the day I learned the meaning of *heartbreak*. How could she, knowing that I was planning to marry him and have his babies?

All at once, my fragile feminine ego dealt with the loss of trust for my most cherished friend. The one I'd allowed to read treasured passages in my diary, not to mention her teaching me how to stuff my pathetic first bra with three layers of tissue. She broke the news in the girl's locker room after gym while I stuffed a wad of powder pink Kleenex into the second deflated cup. I used it to blow my nose instead.

Suddenly, I hated Jeffrey for saying yes and having the nerve to suggest that I ask his best friend, Ralph, to the dance so we could double-date in Ralph's car. And I'm embarrassed to admit that's exactly what I did. I thought it would be a chance to look fantastic, smile incessantly, and show my pride. I was wrong. Instead, I had a miserable time watching Rona and Jeffrey dance the night away. Ralph was so tall, I got a stiff neck just talking to him. On the way home, I heard heavy breathing and the rustling of Rona's crinolines in the backseat. I didn't dare turn around, so I bit the inside of my cheeks until they bled.

Sadly, my special friendship with Rona disintegrated into something superficial. It was hard to look at her. Instead, my eyes were riveted to the bluish marks on her neck. After we graduated, she wrote me very descriptive letters from college about her several sexual encounters. A few years later, she showed up at my wedding in a dress cut down to her navel. She had become a siren, while I was still a virgin.

As a naïve young bride, I became increasingly paranoid, watching my new friends carefully at dinner parties, following them into the kitchen as they helped my husband clear the dishes. The man I had chosen as my husband was charming and amicable, but what I really wanted were sisters, women whose company I could enjoy, women whom I could trust. But it was rare to find women who maintained the same demeanor around a man. In amazement, I observed my new so-called girlfriends as they turned into totally different creatures . . . voices lowered, fingers pulling strands of hair over a sultry eye.

Watch out echoed through my subconscious as I began keeping an eye on my man. If only I could have said, "I need your loyalty" to the friend, and "I need to trust you" to the man.

Eventually, my fear of betrayal became a self-fulfilled prophecy, and after eight years of marriage, I divorced. I heard through the grapevine that Rona, too, was divorced. Now we were on an equal plane. It took a great deal of work and introspection to lose this mental picture of myself as a wounded bird, a victim of deceit. When I finally did, I felt free to try to love again.

Now I'd lay the ground rules early in all my relationships. I surrounded myself with hardworking career women like myself who were dedicated and constantly juggling family and business. I finally found women who needed to share their failures as well as their successes. Socially, I gravitated toward couples who respected and admired one another, relationships that seemed to strike a healthy balance.

But the most important thing that I did for myself was to bring past jealousies and insecurities out of the closet. No matter how deeply rooted, I would no longer feel guilty over having those feelings. I was finally freed from the past.

There are many times when attractive women, maybe stewardesses, waitresses, or saleswomen, have ignored me completely, falling all over my man with charming smiles that could give you an instant cavity. But instead of feeling threatened, I have blatantly pointed this out to him. I've shown him that some women are simply not good sisters. Sometimes he'll reluctantly give in to the truth of what he sees; that always relaxes me and makes me feel loved and very, very sane. He might even laugh when I begin singing the first few lines of "Lord Help the Sister."

Sandi's story was written after she came to terms with her deep fear of betrayal and the guilt she felt, which was related to the fear. "When I stopped hiding my fear of being betrayed and shared it with my loved ones, not only did I learn that others had similar feelings but my anxiety lessened. This ultimately resulted in less tension and more trust within my friendships, and my marriage."

Sandi has been remarried for twenty-two years and has two daughters and a grandson.

Motherhood

The Sacred Portal

Paula Hawkins

It was late into the evening on June 9, 1978, that I gave birth to a buoyant, bright-eyed baby boy. The pregnancy had gone well, but with some soul-stirring awareness, due to an onerous and distressing event, about bringing a child into the world with the absence of a father. I knew at 11:03 P.M., on that early-summer night in 1978, that I would pledge myself to the comfort and well-being of this precious life to the best of my ability. My maternal instincts kicked in like a steamroller.

At the time, I was very involved in the business world and found it quite a juggling act to fulfill the roles of mother, nurturer, and provider, not to mention chief cook and bottle washer. When my son was in grade school, I authorized myself to take a vital step (leap, if you will) of passage into motherhood: I abandoned my career! I began my own business to enable my presence in the home at the end of the school day.

These years of motherhood have been glorious and dreary, blessed and grievous, gratifying and frustrating, serene and worrisome. I grew up when I became a mother. I began peeling away my own shallow facade. I grew deeper and more in tune with reality and truth. I have been stretched, expanded, protracted, and literally pushed to the limits in my own growth. I am frequently awed at how my own son "grew me up."

I am especially amazed at the beauty I have come to embrace in the paradoxes of life. It is inconceivable to know true serenity if you haven't endured worry; gratification if you haven't weathered frustration; grandeur without dreariness; sanctity without grief. I've learned to embrace it all — the good with the bad, the prize with the defeat. To shun the difficult and only embrace the comfortable can only stifle and derail the pilgrimage.

With motherhood came a deepening and wakening into my own profound depths of realness and authenticity.

Having witnessed life's paradoxes in my son, and embracing them all, I am more in tune and accepting of the paradoxes in my own life, and in the lives of those I have the privilege to come in contact with. I am less judgmental and more nurturing. I've learned to shut up and listen more often. In times of adversity, I have learned to be still and come back to the quiet, sanctified place within myself that settles and silences the clamor of my mind — that still, small voice.

Today, my son is a senior in high school, and I have achieved another right of passage: the right to give some of that time and energy back to myself. This passage seems to be one of moving through the same gateway, headed in a different direction. Passing through this portal, regardless of the direction, launches a pilgrimage of frustration and adversity, hellos and good-byes, as well as jubilation and contentment. I feel equivocally blessed and inspired to have had the privilege and benefit to pass through this sacred portal.

Paula hopes that through her story she can relieve some of "the isolation and loneliness of single parents." She feels her experience of motherhood has deepened her spirituality and made her a wiser and more real individual.

Paula's son has now graduated from high school.

Motherhoodless

Jennie M. Maloney

Lately, I find that I am torn between lamenting my lack of motherhood and celebrating the absence of the responsibility and turmoil that children create in the lives of their parents. Until recently, every time an infant or toddler wandered across my path, I became distressed by the recurring thought that I should be "married with children" by now. Somehow, I began to appreciate the snuggles and hugs I received from my nieces and nephew, without simultaneously having to choke back my craving for a child of my own. I began to realize that I could enjoy my afternoons or evenings of play with other people's children, and then leave the major child-rearing chores to their parents. Now on days when that nagging child lament seeps into my brain, I whisper to myself that the snuggles I often long for from flesh of my flesh, bone of my bone, are often the exception to the rule in the child-adult interaction game, and that the ratio of snuggles to struggles is probably one to fifty.

Every parent I know ends a frustrating child-rearing story with a caveat about how rewarding and "worth it" parenthood is. Yet sometimes, during moments when I sit comfortably on my couch, idly reading the Sunday papers with my feet up, I can't help wondering, How worth it is worth it? The truth is that even though I'm not where I thought I would be at this point in my life, I'm happy. How many people can say that? Okay, so I don't fit into the glossy magazine advertisements of mommy and daddy and baby. I know I should be sad and lonely without these other dimensions in my life, and I am sad and lonely sometimes. There are times when I see a mother pushing a carriage across a street, or a group of parents watching toddlers play T-ball, and I can't help but cry for a child of my own to take to tumble school or swimming lessons. Yet, I can comfort myself with the knowledge that those who do have children cry sometimes from the stress they create. We all cry sometimes. Everyone has sad and lonely days or frustrating days. Nothing is perfect. My father often tells me that if you have more good days than bad days, you are way ahead in the game. Right now, that makes me feel like an Olympic gold medalist.

I have grown to learn that even though sometimes it seems as though everyone around me is coupled and parenting, or on their way to parenting, being single and childless has a lot of advantages. Perhaps I'm calmer now because I'm reaching the age where my window of opportunity to have children is slowly closing. Maybe my mental window is starting to close on the idea of children. It's as if the fish-or-cut-bait time is getting closer and closer; sitting in the shade cutting bait or drifting in the bow of the boat and taking in the sights has begun to look better than actually getting up and fishing. At times, I think it will honestly be a relief when the window is closed and the choice is over.

For now, motherhoodlessness is not the worst state in the world to live in. Once you box up the childhood dreams and dolls and put them on a shelf in the back of the closet, there is more room for other opportunities in life. There is the freedom to take advantage of spontaneous over-night adventures, make elaborate travel plans, and treat myself to expensive dinners. I have time to leisurely cook dinner, read books, and relax in long bubble baths. Time for tennis lessons, golf, bicycle rides, and walks. The phone rings, and if I am not already out, or on my way out, I am available. When I do stay home, it's a peaceful, meditative environment. I've found that once you let go of the idea that your life is lacking something, you give yourself the freedom to enjoy the things you do have. It's a free and liberating experience. Although celebrating motherhoodlessness is often in the lead in the race for the spotlight in my circus of emotions, lamenting the lack of children in my life keeps edging toward center stage, and at times I can still hear my biological alarm clock ringing and ringing and ringing. Lately, though, when the alarm goes off, I reach deep inside, press the snooze button, and just kick back and enjoy my life the way it is a little bit longer.

Jennie was prompted to write this story by the fact that she was thirty-six years old and most of her friends and family were married and had children. Jennie told me, "I realized that I was trying to live life within the framework of those around me. I maintained a home, entertained, and socialized with couples and children, waiting for the missing pieces in my life to appear." Slowly, she began to change her lifestyle, travel more, and take advantage of the freedom that being single and childless allowed. "I began to feel whole on my own, and enjoyed my life the way it was, and I wanted to share my newfound appreciation with others." Since writing this story, Jennie has married the "man of her dreams." She says, "I truly believe that in letting go and enjoying life, life gave me back what I needed. As far as motherhood is concerned? Let's see what life has in store."

Unconditional Love

Carol Hutt

A phone call on October 24, 1987, began one of the saddest periods of my life. The caller was my thirty-two-year-old son in New York City, telling me that he had been ill and unable to work for two weeks. The cause, AIDS. I was dumbstruck and heartstruck all in one instant.

I had suspected he was living an alternative lifestyle, but we had never discussed it. His homosexuality was difficult for me to comprehend, but I accepted it, for my love has no bounds when it comes to my children.

I have no doubt my son was painfully aware that announcing that he was gay would have a shocking effect upon his conservative family. So he simply avoided its mention.

Immediately following his college graduation, he moved to Boston, then to New York. The sophistication, excitement, and cultural advantages of city life had always attracted him and he very much seemed to enjoy it.

When he returned home for visits, it was always a time of great celebration, although we always wished he could come more often and stay longer. We were to learn later that he could not afford to do so because of high medical bills. But he seemed healthy and happy, and we never suspected.

He then spent two years in Hawaii, returning to New York in June 1987. We spoke often on the phone, and he always seemed to have a cough. But he attributed it to a cold that was "just hanging on."

His plans were to work a few months, then come home for Christmas, something we all looked forward to with great anticipation. Then came the October phone call with all its dreadful implications. I will treasure forever the memory of the sound of pure blessed relief in his voice as I told him he must come home immediately so that we might care for him.

He had seen others with the disease, disowned by their families and treated as outcasts, with nowhere to go but to charity hospitals, and they were dying. We were soon to learn that Tom had encephalitis, one of the many opportunistic diseases that can strike AIDS patients. He was exhausted and weak and unable to pack his belongings and fly home unassisted. So my husband and another son flew to New York a few days later, packed his things, and the three of them arrived home on October thirty-first.

His relief and delight in being home was touching and beautiful to see. He felt safe and loved and accepted within the bosom of his family. I delighted in cooking his favorite foods, and he ate heartily. During his last days in New York, he had little energy to prepare meals or go out to eat. Now, at home, he ate with great relish.

But his body was deteriorating with each passing day, and after only twelve days at home, he was to spend the last two months of his life in the hospital.

I spent ten to twelve hours of each day at his bedside, and the rest of the family came regularly. Tom spoke very little, but he was totally aware and delighted in our presence. Christmas came and I grieved that there was no gift I could give him, no celebration that he could attend.

On January eleventh, a nurse informed me the end was near. Our family gathered in his room for the last time, leaving quietly around midnight. I stayed, lying in a bed opposite his. His eyes seemed never to waver from my face throughout the night. Once I smiled and waved at him and he grinned and attempted to wave back. Around 6:00 A.M., his breathing became heavy and labored, till about 10:00 A.M., when it slowly stopped.

It had finally happened, but it still seemed impossible and unreal to me. I was to grieve deeply for several months, punishing myself over and over again for not having been able to help him live. In my mind, he had come home for help and I had been unable to give it. But slowly, slowly, new thoughts began to seep into my thinking.

It had been obvious that he was at peace with himself. He had known and accepted that he was going to die. But he wanted to be with his family when this happened. He needed to know that we loved him as much as we always had and that we accepted him exactly the way he was. We gave him this assurance and our love surrounded him in a halo of protection. He died with a sweet smile upon his face.

When I asked Carol how she coped with the experience, she told me, "No matter how old your children are, you still have a protective instinct. I wanted him to know it was all right. A person's sexuality is only a part of who they are. My son was so funny, good, and creative." She said it all happened so quickly and it was so all-consuming, she didn't have time to think. She wanted him to feel loving acceptance, and make him comfortable.

Are You His Grandma or His Mom?

Barbara Kois

We had just finished lunch when the bomb dropped. Present were my sons Andrew, five, and Steve, three, and Andrew's friend Brandon. I hadn't a gray hair showing, thanks to my hairdresser, and yet, as they ran out to play, Brandon said with childlike candor, "Andrew, your mom looks like a grandma!"

I raced to the mirror and inwardly wailed, How could he? I had been trying to believe that no one noticed my age; that everyone presumed I was the same age as the other school mothers, and that maybe I had spent a lot of time in the sun, hence my extra wrinkles.

Brandon's statement was a blow. I had once been asked by an elderly lady, "Are these your grandchildren?" When I replied with a devastated "No," she quickly apologized for confusing me with someone else. I wrote her off as a confused person probably, with poor eyesight, and I forgot about the incident — until Brandon shattered my wishful thinking once and for all.

When a friend subsequently asked me to be the coordinator for Grandparents' Day at

94

school, I decided to laugh and be happy in my "predicament," and to encourage other Older Mothers of Little Kids (OMLKs) to do the same. OMLKs are defined as women forty or older, with one or more offspring forty inches or under.

When I was having my babies at ages thirty-five, thirty-seven, and thirty-nine, I gave no thought to how old I'd be when they graduated from high school, college, got married, bore my grandchildren, and had their midlife crises. But when my Steve is forty-three, I'll be eighty-three, or already gone.

I used to believe that ten years' difference was nothing; that age is all in your mind.

Ten years — a decade. Considering that we get six, seven, or, at most, eight or nine decades, one is certainly significant and not to be treated lightly. Think how decades change things: At two, we're in diapers; at twelve, many girls are in bras; at twenty-two, we're finishing college; at thirty-two, we may have multiple children and even multiple marriages under our belts. At forty-two, speaking for myself only, I finally grew up. At fifty-two, aging is well in process; perhaps grandmotherhood and maybe menopause have arrived. By sixty-two, we're retiring, and yet I foolishly thought that a decade didn't matter, as if I had dozens of them left.

But being older has its positive aspects, as well. I am inspired to try to look my best, exercise, be energetic, and participate actively with my kids and their friends. I want to be young at heart, to empathize with childlike views. I have learned that "this, too, shall pass," so I don't treat minor things as catastrophes.

The benefits also include having two groups of friends: my peers, who have high school- and college-age kids, and then my kids' friends' parents, who are younger than I.

It's not that I ever wish my children were older. I just wish I were younger and had more years ahead of me. I turned forty when Steve, my third child, was three months old. Forty was a shock. As never before, I glimpsed the brevity of life — I saw those decades rushing past. I knew in a different and painfully realistic way that one day my life would end, that it was probably more than half over, that in twenty short years I'd be (gasp!) sixty! I saw the toll that time, pregnancies, fifty pounds gained and lost each of three times, and just life itself had taken. Reality was setting in.

After grasping the seriousness of the age matter, I realized that there was but one course to take: I bought Kathy Peel's book — entitled *Do Plastic Surgeons Take Visa?* — ordered youth-giving vitamins, started exercising, stocked up on antiaging creams, and decided that I was headed for the *Guinness Book of World Records* as the "Only Woman in the World to Bear All of Her Three Children Between the Ages of Thirty-five and Thirty-nine."

Although I admit that the fading of the outer shell (my body) pains me greatly, I know this is a wrong emphasis. I have chosen to focus instead on enjoying these precious and fleeting days with my young children. At my age, I know how quickly time flies. I'll blink and the kids will have gone to college and how old I am won't really matter. But the memories I made with them will. So I'm putting on my Rollerblades and trying to be the very best mother I can be at every age.

Barbara believes that having had her children at a later age has provided a precious opportunity. "I don't feel like I missed out on anything, or feel, What could I be doing now if I didn't have children? I had a full life before I had my children." She feels another advantage is that when you are older, you realize how quickly time passes and you tend to enjoy even the small tasks, which could have seemed tedious when you were younger.

Beyond the Looking Glass

Marlena Thompson

While growing up, I never thought too much about parenthood. I suppose this was partly due to the fact that I came of age during the late sixties and seventies, a time when it was trendy for twenty- and thirty-somethings to behave as if they were in an extended period of adolescence. Also, the parameters within which womanhood had traditionally been defined were expanding, both rhetorically and in reality. The fact that my own childhood was still a source of painful memories very likely contributed to my initial fear and distaste about the idea of parenthood. In any case, not once during the five years of my first marriage, while I was in my early to mid-twenties, did I even consider the possibility of motherhood.

That changed after I married again — this time to a man who already had four children from two previous marriages. Perhaps it was the fact that having children bound him to other women that made my own motherhood so urgent an ambition. Or perhaps it was that, once in a relationship within which I felt cared for, I felt the intense need to nurture.

As often happens, ironically, to women who've spent much of their adult lives practicing one form of contraception or other, pregnancy didn't happen overnight. It took me over a year to get pregnant — and when I did, I received the news joyfully. I knew I would have a daughter from the moment I discovered there was a child in my womb. I know people scoff at such intuitive knowledge, but I also know that it exists. My daughter was an embryonic dynamo, reacting strongly — and visibly — to the loud and bombastic classical music I favored at the time. This was no ordinary child, of that I was sure.

I was right, but I wouldn't learn just how extraordinary she was until much later.

It wasn't so much I who gave birth to Jenny as it was Jenny who determinedly pushed her way out into the world only an hour and a half after I — we — arrived at the hospital. The doctor commented that he'd never seen a newborn so alert, so eager to take in the sights of her new surroundings, belying the belief at the time that all babies are born blind.

I felt that I was complete — and it wasn't until the moment of Jenny's birth that I understood why. For now I would have a confidante. My daughter and I would talk. And talk. And talk. I had never had that kind of relationship with my own mother. Conversations that involved feelings — dreams or demons — did not form a part of the fabric of my childhood. And I craved them still.

So when Jenny still didn't talk after three years of developing precociously in every other area, I began to worry. Not worry — panic. At four, Jenny was yet to engage in the prattle typical of children newly able — however simply — to report their impressions of a freshly discovered world. There were also other telltale neurological signs that indicated all was not well. It was apparent that Jenny was . . . different. In fact, I held on to that adjective long after it ceased to mean much, because it was infinitely easier to accept than that other word describing Jenny — *autistic*.

Autism is a syndrome of neurological abnormalities that impair sensory perception, ways of relating to others — and the use of language.

Irony of ironies: This daughter of mine, whom I had prematurely — and selfishly — cast in the role of confidante, could be no such thing. I was humbled — and given an early lesson (learned sooner or later by all parents) in the futility of playing director in the real-life dramas that are our children's lives.

But that painfully acquired knowledge helped me to accept and cherish Jenny exactly as she is. The more she developed into her own person, the more the behaviors, symptomatic of autism, became simply characteristics of her own special self. Indeed, I came to realize that I was right in sensing her uniqueness while I was still pregnant with her. Autistic people are hypersensitive to sensory stimuli. I hadn't just imagined Jenny rollicking rhythmically in my womb — she had danced! Nor had the doctor imagined Jenny's incredible attentiveness at birth — she *had* been taking it all in, storing up all that visual information for possible use at a later time.

My Jenny, whose remarkable sense of color is a testament to the gifted autist's supersensory perception, has proven herself to be a true artist. It was while watching her work, oblivious to the product she was creating but totally absorbed in the process of creation, that I had an epiphany. I realized that in knowing my daughter and coming to terms with who she really is, I have come to know myself. For by ceasing to look to her to compensate for a childhood bereft of intimacy, I have been forced to look inward and accept responsibility for and cherish who I am, regardless of my parents' deficits or my child's limitations. And by embracing imperfection, my own most of all, I have stopped defining my daughter by any label, autistic or otherwise. For it is impossible for me to imagine her being any different from the way she is — perfectly endearing in her imperfection — and the perfect daughter for me.

Jenny is now a teenager, and Marlena is beginning to see her as an "almost adult" who has a life to live without mama's constant supervision. Marlena was sixteen when her father died, and that was when she began seeing her mother as a woman, not just a mom.

Marlena has a series of children's poems being published, and is a singer/storyteller "because stories are what life is all about."

Stand Up, Mothers!

Marlynn Peron

The moment he uttered the words, I knew there would be no turning back. We had crossed a line. Everything would be measured by before and after that moment. Instantly ancient is how I felt, no longer able to feel young again. Whatever I responded would be crucial. This remark would make or break our relationship. We sat there, not speaking, the two of us. I wanted to run, to scream, to sob: *No! No!* Fragments of thought flew across my consciousness. Would his father turn his back on him? Would his brothers hate him? Would he be left out? My once-upon-a-time baby is gay! Fiercely, I wanted to protect him; never let anyone or anything hurt him. I barely breathed audibly, "You are very brave to tell me this."

"I am gay." I envisioned my boy dressed in women's clothing, luring small children. I was frightened beyond any fear previously in life. Instant guilt washed over me — it must be my fault, I thought — a whole list of "if only." Mothers are quick to assume responsibility, quick to focus on themselves and their wants and wishes.

The enormous fear of the moment was to keep

the secret. Let us not tell anyone just yet. I feared no one would love my boy. My fear overrode my child's needs and feelings.

It did not take my husband long to see an overwhelming sadness within me. In time, he figured it out for himself. He approached the situation with two choices: We love our boy for who he is or we lose him. We chose love.

As for the rest of the world, we no longer care what they think. We do not announce our heterosexual children; we need not announce our homosexual child. If the knowledge would be of benefit to our child's life, or help another person, we share the information. Our boy has not changed. He is the same boy we always knew and loved; we just know more about him now.

Many unanswered questions from his adolescence now have answers. Why did he always want to be with me? He felt safe and knew he would be loved. Why was he so sad? Why did he cry and say that he did not fit in anymore? The terrible sadness is still there in his life. It is not an easy life, and it's often a lonely one. Certainly a life that costs a lot of dreams.

We firmly believe he was born gay. He did not wake up one day and decide to be gay. I did not cause his gayness. Evil did not draw him into gayness. Think! Did you choose to be straight? Did you decide it one day? Of course you had no choice. Just one day a child and the next day a confused teenage boy having strange night dreams about your friends. It is a frightening world to wake up to, and he deserves all the love and encouragement available.

Our children ask two things of us in life: One is to love them unconditionally; the other is to be proud of them. If you deny your child, do you love him? Is the cost of what someone else might think worth more to you than your child? Even though I know gay young male friends of my son and am friends with their mothers, not one mother has spoken openly to me. Why must this remain a secret, a shameful thing? Why do this to a child? What is there to *fear?* Stand up, mothers, and count for your child.

When Marlynn's son first told her he was gay, she was afraid of what other people might think, and feared that someone might hurt him. But, over time she learned, "education chases away fear. Gay is nothing to fear; gay is no reason to be ashamed." In all the years since, not one woman has spoken to her of a gay child. She attempted to gather a support group for mothers of gay children in the community, and not one person attended. By writing this story, Marlynn hopes to motivate these mothers to stand by their gay sons (or daughters) and be proud of them. "They are not broken; they do not need fixing."

Hard Lessons

Christina Keenan

My children aren't little anymore. My son has to lean down to kiss me good-bye before school. And when I have a chat with my daughter, she can stand in front of me and look me squarely in the eye. Sometimes when I am upset, they will actually encourage me to place my head on *their shoulders!*

So here I am, a mother of teenagers, and it is only recently that it has begun to dawn on me that I am living what is left of their young adulthood. Sometimes this thought overwhelms me with grief so deep that it is hard to think of anything else. It all seems to have gone so fast, too fast, really. At this point in time, I can only look back and wish I could bring the memories a little closer, so I could feel them.

As a mother, I think each of us gets caught up in the bigger picture of our children's lives, and it takes so long to realize that it is all the small moments that really matter. I grieve now for all the lost small moments, and all the things I won't do again. In my heart's journal of small moments are the nights rocking them, burying my face in their necks, breathing in their fragrance. Holding their hands to cross the street, reading to them at night, and giving them baths. I used to go into their rooms late at night to watch them sleep, cover them up, and give them one final kiss good night.

The other day, I found a copy of *Black Beauty* under my bed with the bookmark still in it from the last time I read to them. It truly was the last time, and I remember thinking, I didn't know it was the last time I would ever read to them when I put the book down that night. Part of me wished I had known; then another part wondered how that information would have made me feel. Would I have been happy or sad to have had this knowledge?

Looking back now, my vision is twenty-twenty, and time seems to have gone so fast. But in reality, we give up our children to the world small moment by small moment. The mother's love that I feel for them, however deep and profound, has to grow toward separation, and this is a hard lesson to learn. I have to force myself not to be afraid that my world seems smaller as their world grows larger. My head and heart will always be full of them. It is only my house that will feel empty. I sometimes wonder if the lessons we teach our children are as valuable as the ones we learn from them.

I guess now would be a good time to remember that we never really lose our children; *they just grow up.* Small moment by small moment, it is only their childhood that is gone. It is sometimes hard not to confuse this thought.

Now I have teenagers, and it all seems to be going by in a blur, as well! But I'm lucky to have learned a hard lesson — to cherish and file away each small moment because that is all there is. I still have quite a few small moments left. I still have to hide their Christmas presents; they still beg me to bake cookies; they still help me decorate the Christmas tree; and when they are hurt or sick, they still call for me.

We are all under the same roof, and if I need to, and I need to a lot, I can still go into their rooms late at night and watch them sleep. I can cover them, and I can still give them one final kiss good night.

For this, I am truly grateful.

Christina is a registered nurse when she is not spending time with her husband and children or writing. She is a prolific writer and has won several literary awards. "Much of my work embodies women's issues, and motherhood, although it is not limited to this category. As a writer, I try to find the common ground. Emotion is my link, and if the reader responds on a deep emotional level, then I've done what I've set out to do."

From
One
Generation
to
Another

The Meatloaf Mirror

Debbie Oyama

I remember the day it hit me, the fact that I had become my mother. I was making a meatloaf for dinner when I suddenly got this surge of creativity. I used cherry tomatoes for eyes and a carrot for the nose. My meatloaf man had parsley hair and onion teeth. It wasn't until I added the finishing touch of catsup dripping from the nose and mouth that I stood staring in disbelief. As I gazed upon the face of Meatloaf Man, I felt as if I were looking into a mirror and Mom was staring back at me. She had warned me this would happen.

My mother is an artist who delights in turning the most mundane household chores into opportunities to express herself. Once, when Dad was out of town on business, she painted a six-foot purple cow on the kitchen wall. Vacuuming, dusting, and sweeping were just excuses to turn the volume up on the stereo and shake her bootie, something I find myself doing more often than I care to admit.

There were little signs over the years leading up to this moment, like when my son came home crying over a scraped knee. "Put some spit on it," I advised. When I was on the phone and the kids

111

thought that was the only time they could communicate with me, I asked them, "Is this a carrot in my ear?"

Of course, in the back of my mind, I knew I had heard those words spoken to me straight out of my own mother's mouth, but I quickly pushed it further back in my head. As time went on, though, it became more difficult to deny what was happening to me.

I was driving my girls to high school one day and I started singing along with Hootie and the Blowfish on the radio in my best operatic voice. "Oh, Mom, that is so Memère," they complained. (Memère is what they call my mother.) I'll strike up a conversation with someone if I'm standing in a long line, and my kids will say, "You're just like Memère. You tell your whole life story to some stranger in the grocery store." When other people start to notice these things, you just have to admit it. Even then I'd say, "I know; I was just doing that to be funny."

Then I began to speak my mother's language. I get the weirdest looks from my friends when I ask, "Scupp Scoffee, anyone?" That's my mother's way of asking if anyone wants coffee. If I'm going out for the evening, it's not jewelry I put on; it's baubles.

When I was a teenager, Mom embarrassed me to tears by performing the potato-bug dance in front of my friends. She learned it from a local children's television show. It looks a lot like the Pee-wee Herman dance, with a bit more arm movement. Guess what I did at my daughter's eighteenth birthday party? Yep, the potato-bug dance!

Now that I've accepted this transformation that has been taking place all of my life, I've come to the conclusion that it's not such a bad thing. The truth is, I've always admired my mother. I realized, too, that most of my friends have found themselves in the same boat.

One evening not long ago, the women in our family got together for a girls' night out at my sister's house. As I watched my two daughters doing the potato-bug dance with the rest of us, I thought to myself, I should warn them. "Girls," I would say, "one day you will look into the face of your meatloaf and see me staring back at you!"

Debbie, forty-two years old, is a housewife and has three teenagers. She also publishes a monthly newsletter called The Meatloaf Monthly *and is a volunteer adviser for* Bear Essential News for Kids. *Debbie says, "I knew other women would relate to this story because most of us become our mothers in some way, and it's not such a bad thing."*

And Mommy
Wouldn't Help

Debbe Andrews

The first time,
    I was four.
It didn't hurt too bad —
    and he was my new daddy.
He told me it was our secret,
    only ours.
And I would be naughty —
    if I told anyone.

A few days later,
    I almost did.
He knew —
    and showed me a gun.
It was for our protection,
    you know.
Because sometimes —
    naughty people have to be shot.

Day after day,
    I hoped he would stop.
I hid in the closet —
    he found me.
If I was a good girl,

or got good grades,
he would surely stop
        He didn't.

I prayed he would stop —
        it happened more.
Was I so bad
        even God wouldn't help?
At twelve, it turned to rape.
        I sat and cried.
And thought, it wasn't so bad before.
        Can we go back to that?

Many times I woke,
        his hand over my mouth.
The house was dark,
        and I tried not to cry.
Mommy caught him one Sunday.
        We went to the hospital.
The police and doctors checked me.
        When we got home, he was gone.

But Mommy couldn't care
        for us kids by herself.
It was too much.
        He was back on Tuesday.
So here I was,
        twelve years old.
Been molested and raped —
        and left to die in my sorrow.
And Mommy wouldn't help.

Now a woman, Debbe is happily married and has four children. She wrote this poem when she was twelve years old. When Debbe was in her early thirties, a judge allowed her to testify against the man who had begun molesting her more than twenty-five years before. He had molested another child. Soon after the trial, Debbe felt the black hole in her soul beginning to shrink. However, she says the nightmares are recurring, but it helps to talk with friends, and her husband, who provides her with tremendous support. Debbe shares her story as a cry for the emancipation of others. "I hope my poem helps other victims become survivors. I hope somehow, someday, someway, it will help the children."

Simple Truths

Maria A. Little

To whom do you owe your success? Amid all the current fads with trendy names like *coaching, mentoring,* and *partnering,* I reflect on a simpler time and think about the person who impacted my life in the most profound way — without all the fuss and bother of a trendy title. This story is dedicated to that extraordinary woman.

She was the oldest of three children and her family lived in Switzerland. When her mother died at an early age, she shouldered the task of caring for her father and two younger brothers at a time when finding enough food was just one small worry in a series of solemn struggles.

After the conclusion of World War II, she pondered opportunities elsewhere in the world, due to her strong wanderlust, as well as a budding relationship that would lead to marriage. Her love for travel took her first to England and then to the United States. She settled in New Jersey, married her Italian immigrant partner, and together they had three children — two sons and a daughter. Having received a business-college education in her home country, she continued to embrace lifelong learning, culminating with her enrollment in a memoir-writing course at age seventy-three at a local community college in Seattle.

As she started her memoirs, her health began to fail, dramatically altering her lifestyle. Congestive heart failure kept this normally vibrant lady at home with frequent medication and continuous oxygen. Despite her acute capacities and an iron will, she left this earth last year at the age of seventy-six. Her passing marked the end of a splendid era.

Bertha Roth never won celebrity status or political recognition and she never received any awards or medals. She didn't earn any advanced degrees and she never won the lottery. She lived a simple and often difficult life, experiencing the same problems as most contemporary women — the routine dilemmas that accompany child rearing, working, managing family finances, and enduring a divorce. She also encountered obstacles many of us cannot even imagine: raising two younger brothers at the age of nineteen; surviving the hunger and devastation of World War II; silently suffering domestic abuse while fiercely protecting her three offspring. This is the Bertha most people didn't know.

The woman most people knew lived in a modest house in New Jersey with her children, feeding family, friends, and neighbors in her humble kitchen and transforming simple excursions, like going out for an ice cream cone, into great adventures.

No one ever noticed that she was fluent in five

languages, that she was licensed as the first woman barber in the state of New Jersey, or that she single-handedly remodeled and repaired her humble home like a master carpenter.

All who knew her loved her wisdom, her straight talk, and her incredible work ethic. When others turned to her for assistance in combating a seemingly unbearable challenge, she would offer compassion and good sound advice. Ever willing to share her deeper perspective, she would calmly dive into a tough predicament. Her proposed solutions always had some universal element of truth and virtue in them and the answers always looked so evident after the fact. Many wondered why they hadn't thought of it themselves.

Her guidance inspired many and taught lessons that could never have been learned in a classroom. In fact, most of her counsel was obtained while sitting at her old gray Formica-topped kitchen table over a cold beer or a cup of coffee. Possessing a knack for getting "back to the basics," she would retrieve with her good common sense lost souls who had gone astray. Her words were always straight and to the point. "Respect others. Do no harm. Think before you speak or act. Listen to your heart. Identify and perfect your purpose in life and then remain true to it. Have fun. Dance often, and sing even if you're off-key."

How she used to dance. She would two-step her way around her little kitchen with its old white metal cabinets and faded linoleum floor, even though she didn't have much to dance about. She was working in a sweatshop while her children attended school, sewing piping in pajamas and making ladies' hats for twenty-five cents a dozen at a time when a loaf of bread cost twelve cents. Still, her simple truths are words to live by.

Now as I sift through the memoirs she wrote and the cards and letters she sent to me, I realize how profoundly she affected my life and how thankful I am that she was there. And better yet, I realize that years from now I still will never cease to learn from this remarkable woman, who was my mother.

Maria's mother made enormous sacrifices to provide her three children with an education that would prepare them for the future and allow them to contribute to others. "It's only fitting that I should share her incredible wisdom with the world," says Maria. "Throughout my life, my mother was a constant source of love and inspiration, and one of my fondest wishes is to be as profound an influence on my son."

Maria holds a master's degree in adult education and training and certification as a professional in human resources. She is currently a training manager and human resources development consultant in the Pacific Northwest.

Revelations

Karen M. Masullo

Part 1

I have heard it said
that first memories are traumatic in nature.

My own experience bears this out.

I have no need to spend thousands of dollars for
    the psychiatric privilege of womb regression,
    however. . . .
The mind performs as it does for good reason
    and I will not violate the vault.

The scene
(as best I can recall)
has me suspended by my ankles;
I am being shaken — first up and then down
    again.
(I am giddy with the fun of this.)
I have swallowed two marbles and a nickel. . . .

Or perhaps, it is the other way around, as I have
    always been partial to change.

There is a woman, giving direction.

For many years I have assumed this to be my
    mother.
My siblings, though, tell me that most of my
    memories involve not my mother
but a succession of well-meaning baby-sitters
    and neighbors.

I find this revelation sad yet shed no tear.

Rather, I force my mother to pay for my self-
    imposed deception at those rare times when
    she does indeed appear.

I am wonderfully skilled at being angry with her.
I stab her with my pen.
These very words — edged in steel — are meant
    to draw blood.

And I dance in the wine from her wounds
    with bacchanalian glee.

I find fault with the very air she dares to breathe
    and shrink from it as if its invasiveness will
    infect me with whatever poison I deem she
    spews.
I am expert at destroying her.
As well I should be;
I studied my technique for many years at the foot
    of the master — my father.

Do not assume that I am without compassion for
    her.

I simply have no patience and, somehow, have
   convinced myself superior to her for this.

Ahh . . . but we are the parents of our children's
   poverty of soul and they mirror our
   indifference.

Part 2

Still . . . I hear the echoes
footsteps fading in the shadows
so clearly instructing me to be unlike her.

Yet here I sit. . . .

Touching keys as once did she,
resting on hips that match her own.

My faults,
emphasized.

My hands are her hands. . . . My face . . . my
   face is her face.

We keep our vaults full of the same memories,
locked with the same stubborn determination.

And I know that we think about each other. . . .
   All of the time.

Karen left home, feeling like a "nobody," when she was fourteen, lived on the streets, and did what it took to survive. "This poem is to my mother, whom I met again at eighteen after being separated from her at the age of four. In the words of Vonnegut, 'and so it goes.'" Karen is now thirty-nine and has been married for eighteen years. She owns a resumé and writing consulting business and volunteers her time speaking to women in crisis and transitions. As for that "nobody special person," she says she is gone.

Pondering

Linda Lorenzo Modica

As my mind wanders down memory lane, I'm floating to a place back in time. Suddenly, I'm making mud pies, being sure to mix in the tiny green leaves, giving the impression that this was parsley. Dressed in a little white sundress, white socks, and my white patent-leather shoes from Easter. Amazingly, not one speck of dirt was on anything other than my vigorous working hands. When I was finished, I excitedly told my little friend that I was going to show my mother my mud pies. I carefully arranged them on the toy dishes and half-ran to present them to my mother, who was hanging clothes in the yard. She told me they were absolutely beautiful, and good enough to eat. I remember I was bursting with pride. It meant so much to me that she thought they were good enough to eat. What a wonderful feeling to be that proud.

Everything I ever did, or ever made, was beautiful, according to her. I couldn't wait to give her presents, because I knew how much she loved everything I did. Each time, I tried to make things even better than the last time, because I always wanted to please her, and hear praise on how good I was at what I did. And, needless to say, I got just that. As a result, I turned out to be a pretty creative person, one who believes in herself.

Funny, though — my mother thinks I have only bad memories.

The most comforting moment in most people's lives is when they're very, very sick and someone is taking care of them. The first thing you think of when you're that sick is that you are going to die. Then a gentle hand touches your fevered brow and soft lips kiss your forehead. Each time you awake from your feverish dream, the smiling eyes that are never weary are gazing down at you, letting you know that you're not alone, not for one minute. Medicine so powerful is a mother's touch. As a result, I turned out to be a very caring and compassionate person.

Funny, though — my mother doesn't see it.

Floating to another place in time, there are many Christmas presents always piled under the tree. How could this be when we were so poor? My mother had a way — layaway. And, I might add, where there's a will, there's a way. We always had nice clothes, my brothers and I. My mother always wore the same things, interchanging them to look different every time. She still had things from twenty years ago, still looking new. She didn't care as long as we had nice things, and we were happy and feeling good about how we looked. As a result, I learned how to persevere. I learned patience and hope, and that all things are possible. I became an unselfish person, who never feels a loss when giving something up to someone else.

Funny, though — my mother doesn't see it that way.

Moving on . . . My mother worked an eight-hour day, stopped to grocery-shop, then picked up three grandchildren on her way home to cook endlessly for the holiday the next day. In between, she fed the children, cooked fourteen different things, cleaned the house, and put the grandchildren to bed. Woke in the morning and took them all to church. As a result, I learned how to do ten things at once. I was able to hold down three jobs and go to school, and take care of two children.

These are the gifts you passed on to me. Don't be threatened by them, and never think I don't remember the good things. These are the only things worth remembering. Already I can see the strength in my daughter. And I'm proud. Mom, live for today, and remember yesterday. There is always something to look forward to tomorrow. You still have everything you started out with, plus more. Six extensions of us kids. You were the seed. I will always love you.

Your daughter.

"My story was prompted by a fight my mom and I had. She accused me of having only bad memories growing up. Our lives were not perfect, but I remember how hard she tried to make it good. Ev-

127

erything I am is learned from the example she showed me." Linda believes you can always rise above difficult situations and hardships. "My family and friends are wonderful and they support and encourage me." Linda is married and is the mother of two "great kids." "I guess you can call me a jack-of-all-trades. I'm a crossing guard, hairdresser, counselor, poet, writer, and mother."

The Talisman

Deborah Ketai

The problem with most good-luck charms is that they're "one size fits all" — that is, they supposedly bring good luck to anyone. If you believe (as I do) that you make your own luck, you'll want a talisman that works just for you.

Mine is a ring that I wear on my right index finger. I wear it when I meet with a prospective client, when I give a speech, and especially when I'm nervous about being in unfamiliar surroundings.

Some unknown artisan crafted the ring from a broad strip of indeterminate metal, hammering it into geometric relief and bending it into a semicircular shape. Unassuming, yet somehow elegant, the ring reminds me of my grandmother Birdie, who gave it to me. Its story is that of a woman who made her own luck — and mine.

It was, after all, luck rather than the vagaries of reproduction that caused her life and mine to intersect. Birdie was my grandfather's second wife, not my father's mother.

She grew up in Chicago, the daughter of a Jewish cigar maker. Her early luck consisted of being born into a loving, if financially strained, family. A career woman by necessity, she fell in love with one of her coworkers, my grandfather, whose father, coincidentally, was also a Jewish cigar maker.

As luck would have it, the two fathers knew each other and approved of the match. It was Birdie's first marriage and my grandfather's second. They accepted job transfers to Minneapolis, but eventually returned to Chicago, followed (a mere two decades later) by my father, with his new wife and baby (me) in tow.

Birdie also had the luck of a survivor. She had beaten both tuberculosis and cancer at a relatively young age. Childless herself, she became a perfect grandmother and counted herself lucky to be one, though she always signed my birthday cards with the name Nonny in quotes, as if afraid to presume upon her station.

Nor did she complain when bad luck came to visit . . . and stayed. She spent years taking care of her mother, whose death was closely followed by my grandfather's descent into blindness, depression, and the cancer that eventually killed him.

And when the mourning was over, Birdie decided to travel. She and my grandfather had always lived simply. I don't believe they ever took vacations, other than an occasional trip to New York when my father was living there, or to California after her sister moved away. Birdie's own health was problematic, but she was determined to live whatever years she had left to their fullest.

When she told me of her desire to see new

places, I assumed she intended to tour the United States, maybe visit Canada or Mexico, or possibly take a B'Nai B'Rith tour of Israel. I was totally unprepared for the announcement that she had booked herself on a charter flight to Peru.

The choice seemed wildly out of character for this quiet woman, the least flamboyant of my three grandmothers. Why Peru? "Because I've never been there, and if I don't go now, I never will," she said.

She loved the trip, even when her posttubercular lungs rebelled in the thin Andean air and kept her from visiting Machu Picchu. And she brought me back the ring.

I've taken it places that Birdie never got to see. It soothed my stage fright when I joined a road band, and in the ten years that I was on tour, it saw almost every state in the eastern third of the country.

As time went by, the ring seemed to take on more and more of Birdie's character, even helping me forgive myself when I could not break a performance contract to attend her funeral. And I like to think that I felt a special warmth on my finger, quite apart from Savannah's summer heat, when I wore it to my brother's wedding so that Nonny could be there in spirit. When I came off the road in 1990, Birdie's ring gave me the courage to start my own consulting business. Three years later, I designed a seminar series, Confident Communication in a Changing Business World. I wear the ring whenever I give a seminar. I tell Birdie's story to every group.

I tell the story because I believe that everyone needs what I am lucky enough to have had in my grandmother: a mentor and a talisman. And because, over the years, that ring has come to symbolize something very important to me: a willingness — no, a need — to take risks; in remembering my meek but formidable grandmother, I am inspired to make my own luck.

Deborah originally wrote this story for a competition sponsored by Smithsonian *magazine and America Online, and it took second place. "I indulge my passion for confident communication in several ways: as a consultant who helps entrepreneurs and professionals grow their businesses; as a published writer and poet; and as a performing musician." She manages a message folder for women business owners on America Online. Offline, she draws inspiration from her companion, Chris, with whom she lives happily ever after.*

Tapestry of Self

Jeni Ioanna Passidakis

That day stands crystallized in my memory: the earthy smell of soil, the saltiness of the sea, and the warm kiss of the Greek sun dancing upon my skin. A chord was struck within me, the beginning of some ancient awakening that to this day remains. This is the earth of my ancestors, the place of their birth, I thought. I am part of this lineage, a strand in the tapestry of time, intertwined with all those who have come before me. I stand here, in this place, awakened to my bones like a lightning bolt sent from Zeus. I am forever changed, never to be the same.

My grandmother was the village weaver on the beautiful Mediterranean island of Crete. Of her six children, twenty-one grandchildren, and twenty-seven great-grandchildren, I am the only one who has heard the song of the loom calling. Her legacy handed down to me, and though I am still only a novice, it continues to teach and inspire me deeply. The hand-carved wooden shuttle she used to hold the strands as she wove has been passed on to me like a baton in a race. I contemplate its meaning and symbolism in my life. Where do I go from this point forth? And where have I been? What gifts will I leave?

133

I have come to find that I am also a weaver of words. My life is my tapestry, telling the tales of self. I trace each thread back, honoring the story it holds, a memory all its own. Like a song, it moves me. Like a breath, it both becomes one with and eludes me. A colorful chronicle of love, lost and found, both within and without. Strands of sorrow and threads of ecstasy. Hues of gray and blue from tears cried in both joy and disappointment.

Up close, I notice the details and the rough spots of isolated incidents and personal initiations. Yet when I stand back and gaze at the tapestry of my life, I see the harmony and beauty of a sacred choreography. Shades and patterns intermingling and blending, creating a richness and rhythm of life's experiences, each a precious thread connecting to the next.

Tears transformed through loving and forgiving, embracing and accepting, both myself and others. You do the best you can with the threads at hand, whispers an inner voice in which I sense the presence of my grandmother. Life is a spiral, ever expanding and ascending simultaneously, like the birthing of our galaxy. All events, experiences, and encounters are significant in this splendid mystery that is life, it says.

With every new color or change of pattern, a threshold of being is crossed, a rite of passage. I feel so grateful and so blessed. I am warmed by the reflection that everyone has their own sacred tapestry. I sense where my personal story has parallels and similarities with the tapestry of others. We are more alike than we realize.

A sense of peace and acceptance fills me as I am reminded that our past is not our potential. I move beyond it and into the freedom of the now and the colors at hand. What is it I seek? What are the textures of my dreams? Each quest of self-discovery first begins with asking a question, and the answers are sure to follow.

Growth comes when we are willing to feel the fear and go forward anyway. It is in living on this edge, and stretching beyond the previous point of comfort, that we discover new colors to weave into our tapestry. Anaïs Nin once said, "Life shrinks or expands in proportion to one's courage," and I have found this to be true.

I am reminded of another wise elder. Spider Woman, from the Native American creation myth, wove the world into being from silken threads within her body. Women are the weavers of life. We are all connected to this sacred web. Our body is the loom and our love the many-colored threads upon the warp and weft. I think how we, too, have all the silken threads we need inside of our very beings. This reminds me to stop looking outside for them and uncover the treasures within.

We each have our sacred story, our tapestry of being and becoming. Let us boldly experiment with new colors yet unwoven and realize our highest dreams! It has been said, "Whatever you dream or desire, begin it now! Boldness has ge-

135

nius, power, and magic in it!" Find that magical thread inside of you. Weave yourself into being! Be all you can be and know you deserve the very best in life . . . because you do. And the world also awaits the best of you!

Jeni's grandmother was a very influential and inspiring force in her life. She still feels her grandmother is a mentor "though she's in spirit form." Writing about her grandmother was not only a tribute but an example of how she processes life and its meaning.

A Summer Walk

Erica Johnson

It was a Sunday in the early summer, the air not yet thick with steamy heat. Dinner was over, and everyone had pushed away from the table with a sigh. Once we could move more comfortably, we would take our walk. I was home from college and relishing the feelings of change. I had reached the point where I felt like an adult, even at home, and with my mother and grandmother there, I felt the tangible thread of the generations moving through and around me in its timeless journey. I understood that I was neither first nor last, and never alone.

Finally, we began moving, the mellow air beckoning us. Our matriarch had declared it time to walk, so we began our stately trek up the hill I had so often streaked up when I would bolt from the supper table at the first faint blast of a train whistle. Now my grandmother, frail and shrinking, her back brace an uncomfortable exoskeleton, supported herself on my mother's strong freckled arm. I followed, loosely tethered by time and emotion.

Down the hill and beyond the tracks lay Swede-town and my grandmother's past. She had lived there, the child of a hardworking immigrant family, her father a railroad man, her mother a laundress. Not welcome at the front doors of the rich people who hired her mother, my grandmother would haul her laundry wagon to their back doors. This was the wrong side of the tracks, I realized, the home of the servant class.

The farther we walked into Swede-town, though, the taller Grandma seemed to get, time sloughing off her straightening shoulders, her footsteps lighter. She pointed out the homes of her friends, told how the services at their church were all in Swedish, and then, reminiscent of Miles Standish, explained how she had delivered love notes from my future grandfather to her girlfriend, while dating his brother Glen. She wouldn't be specific about her switch in affections, except to say that Uncle Glen didn't laugh enough. (We Gibsons do have our priorities!)

I couldn't believe how young she seemed. This was not a hobbling old lady; this was a young woman with fire in her eyes, possessing a fierce pride that would move her from this poor neighborhood to a place of esteem in her community, allow her to marry a good man and raise six children comfortably. For the first time, Swede-town came alive for me. I had rarely even thought of it, let alone seen it through someone else's eyes. Now it was a place filled with connections and history; my hill was my grandmother's hill, the same trains rumbling past her house as mine, the ghost of my great-grandfather waving from the caboose.

Our outing was cut short, since Grandma tired easily, and as we headed back up the hill, I watched her become an aging lady, her step tentative, her lean more pronounced, her chatting ended. She was ready to take her place on our front porch and survey her hard-won domain.

I stood in awe as I watched her youth come and go in a single afternoon, age as fleeting as breath. My grandmother had had all the wishes and dreams I had, been in love and changed her mind, all to make me what I am today. Only in the furthest corner of my heart could I imagine that I was now creating a part of my own granddaughter's life. Never had I felt so folded in time, the generations disappearing as we became one life, beginning and ending, in that one moment of a summer afternoon.

Erica is a cofounder of the Society for Sorry Writers, in Ithaca, New York, where she lives with her husband, daughters, and cats. She was trained in rural and medical social work and has begun writing to help her through what she calls her midlife crisis. "I've always wanted to put words to this event. It was awe inspiring to see my grandmother relive her life and become a young woman again."

Life's
Lessons

The Visit

Lisa M. Cheater

"They're not coming," my sister said nervously.
"They'll be here," I replied, and resumed pacing,
pretending to be interested in the university degrees and articles enshrined on the walls. I
thought this would be a good time for a cigarette,
although I was trying to quit. I patted my
pockets, searching for the familiar shape. I located one, and began my quest for a lighter.

"You really should stop that nasty habit,"
Jennie snapped in a rare display of aggression.
"It's very bad for you, and it makes your clothes
smell." She glanced back toward the waiting
room door.

"Yeah, well, you give up your stock in M&M/
Mars, and I'll give up mine in Virginia Slims," I
said bluntly.

Jennie instinctively reached for a pillow to
clutch in her lap. She had once been beautiful.
Now she was almost two hundred pounds, and
was self-conscious and miserable. I lit the cigarette and desperately drew the smoke into my
lungs. My daydreaming was abruptly halted by
the sound of familiar voices.

"Well, better late than never! I swear, your father is slower than Christmas. And then I had to

comb his hair in the back. He never combs his hair in the back, you know."

"Good to see you, too, Mom," I said sarcastically.

"This is a very nice building!" Mom said as she smoothed her hand over the wallpaper. "And they have handicapped parking right out front for me. I thought I'd never make it up —"

"Mother," I interrupted, already sick of her rambling, "you're not handicapped." I took another drag from my cigarette and moved to sit on the arm of a large chair. "Please be good in there, okay?"

"What are you talking about?" Mom spat out. "You wanted us to come up here, and we did exactly as you asked. I don't know why you always have to be so smart-mouthed." She plopped down on the end of the couch. Her expression quickly shifted from disgust to delight. "Oh, honey, this is nice! It's just like the one we saw at Haverty's." Dad moved wordlessly to the couch, settled into the corner, and nodded in agreement.

I sighed and looked down to study the carpet. What a mistake this will be. I had planned this visit for months, paying for it with my own money because I thought it would help. Our family had drifted apart for years, and my sister and I harbored years' worth of resentment toward our parents. All we'd ever needed was their attention. I suppose it could have been worse, but Jennie and I had suffered in relationships since the day we left home.

I was suddenly startled by a strange gurgling sound, and I turned, to see my father's head bobbing over to the right as he drifted off to sleep. Mom was giggling.

"Hello, folks," a voice greeted from across the room. "Sorry you had to wait. I'm Dr. Millstone. Please call me Don." The man walked over to us and shook our hands. I thought he resembled Joe Friday from *Dragnet*. He motioned toward another door in the waiting room. "Please make yourself comfortable."

I was anxious to stake out a prime location in his office, so I sprang up from my perch on the chair like ammo out of a slingshot. Behind me, I could hear Mom groaning as she tried to get up from the couch.

"Oh boy. I can do it, just hold on a minute." She had to rock back and forth in her seat five times in order to work up enough momentum to hoist herself up. "I've got arthritis," she said to Dr. Millstone as she slowly straightened. "I've made a lot of progress, though. You should have seen me last winter! Couldn't even walk. My friends are always telling me how good I look now."

I glanced out into the waiting room as Mom shuffled past the doctor. He nodded and smiled but said nothing. I was appreciative of that.

Dr. Millstone's office was filled with stuffed animals and plants, letters from patients, and books — lots of books. The furnishings were simple, the kind my grandmother used to have. Dad looked around the room, obviously confused. He glanced at the pile of toys and muttered almost inaudibly, "Lord, what kind a place is this?" Jennie found a safe spot on the couch and surrounded herself with pillows. It looked as though she were trying to build a soft-sculpture fortress around herself.

The doctor eased himself into a puffy brown recliner and looked at my family. "Well now, what shall we talk about?"

I looked out the window and saw that rain was beginning to lightly pelt the glass. I was certain it was about to storm.

"My story is a scenario describing an attempt to reconcile generations of dysfunction and contradiction. It is actually about forgiveness, and the acceptance of history as unchangeable." Lisa believes courage is required to address one's family, "and to humbly confront them with complete honesty." Married to a "wonderfully supportive husband," Lisa owns and operates a firm that provides legal and analytical writing services.

Dark Side of Genius

Kimberly Luxenberg

Why do I give in to the beating of my heart? The feeling that fear is inevitable, the end so near? How do you give in to the strength you know exists? To let yourself fight for peace of mind? Do you ever look around at the people you encounter every day? Sometimes you pick out that person who looks like they have their act together. You base that assumption on what they're wearing and whether or not they're smiling. Don't you hate yourself on those days?

Remember being fifteen, when the biggest problem you had was whether or not you should go to second base? Those were the days. Today, it's all about the rent check, another AIDS test, hating your boss, and wondering if your man is really who he says he is. Do you know what it's like to have a manic-depressive for a mother? Picking Mom's head out of the sweet-potato pie made for great Passover conversation.

Is it normal to feel so out of control? Like you're floating through your own existence? When will I stop daydreaming about Mom's funeral? Does happiness fit into the equation that makes up my life? I need more than fleeting moments. Will I ever stop running away from my mind?

147

I wonder what it's like to believe in oneself. Creating a life seems like so much fun. But can the creations of your mind actually play a part in "your" reality?

I remember at seventeen, the height of my creativity, I was writing about endless love and blue skies. Naïveté is definitely underrated. Even at seventeen, I couldn't wait to be twenty. I was always in such a rush. I don't really remember why I was so unpleasant, but even at that tender age, misery found me and decided to stick around and have a cigarette.

Will I ever be one of those girls who thinks she's in a great relationship until she finds her man in bed with her best friend? Will I ever be able to afford a 1959 pink Cadillac convertible? How many people I know will die of AIDS by the time I'm thirty? Will I be one of them? Did I ever think that I would feel anything but misery looking out the glass windows that held my fate? What did come out of my infamous waitressing career were these: great characters for a novel, an appreciation of lobster, a Latino lover, and a serious attitude problem. It's pathetic that my girlfriends and I can have a conversation about nail polish and actually be able to name the colors on our toes.

I tripped on acid one night and found myself watching static on the TV. The pathetic thing was not the fact that I was staring at the blank screen but that my mind had never seemed so clear.

At twenty-one, I couldn't drink enough, like the fact that I was legal made a difference. The only difference between one particular night and the rest was that I woke up naked in bed with my boyfriend and my best friend. He was the love of my life; I fell hard, smacking my head along the way. It must have been a hard hit, because when I woke up a year later, I was bulimic, narcotic-addicted, sex-crazed and AIDS-aware, but, damn it, I felt fantastic.

How many times have you stared out the "open window"? More than once? Life turns into a battle, a game, your mind becomes a wasteland filled with self-incrimination, denial, and *fear!* Fear of everything: yourself, sex, career, life, and the inevitable cancellation of *Designing Women* reruns.

Have you ever seen that person walking down the street talking to herself? Have you ever been that person? I remember the Halloween I chased my boyfriend around the house with a machete. I was twenty-two. Have you ever felt like you're on top of the world, only to wake up the next morning with a bloody nose?

The eighties were great. Expensive clothes, new breasts, nice car. Boy, did I have a serious attitude problem then. I remember having a party and walking out of the bedroom in a coat and nothing else. People were drinking booze and snorting lines on Mom's ten-thousand-dollar glass table. Whose coat was I wearing? And where were Mom and Dad? My brother got arrested that night. Nothing more pathetic than a nice Jewish boy being pulled over because he was too polluted to drive. I wonder how much it cost to keep it under wraps. I got a hundred dollars for my silence.

Have you ever tried to talk a friend out of committing suicide? Did you really think she was going to do it?

Do you remember your first pair of Chucky T's? I do. I was having the greatest sex of my life while tripping on ecstasy. I woke up and found that my car had been stolen and the only things those thieves had left behind were a bra, a pair of Keds, and a Wilson Phillips cassette. Have you ever walked around Manhattan with a $1.25 in your pocket? Have you ever done the walk of shame? If you say no, you're lying. Have you ever been on a philosophical roll and had the person you're talking to ask you to repeat yourself because you've lost him or her?

I feel like a glass of scotch, maybe even a cigar. I'm twenty-four — should I feel like that? Have you ever felt like picking up and leaving your life behind? Wouldn't it be nice to have amnesia for a day?

The night I found out I got my first real job, I celebrated by having frozen margaritas. Instead of dinner, I took a friend home, got naked, rolled around for a while, then passed out in the Korean market while waiting to pay for my turkey sandwich. I was twenty-three.

I never liked eating breakfast. Actually, for a

while I didn't like lunch or dinner, either. You know how hard it is to keep up with your best friend's bulimia when you're living at home with your parents?

I got a speeding ticket and never paid it. Now there's a warrant out for my arrest.

Kimberly says she sometimes "feels as though she has lived one hundred years battling her personal demons." She is now twenty-six years old and is anything but pessimistic. "I have been fortunate to be surrounded by the strength, love, and honesty of my family. I have battled my demons and my family's, as well. My mother has struggled through her own life and, in turn, has given me the tools to grow and express myself."

Focus on Me

Beth A. Stableford

I was alone at the bookstore, and my best friend was six hundred miles away. It still feels odd to go without him to places we used to go to together, and the consequence is that I find myself reacting to situations as I know he would. And if he had been at this store with me that day, he would have laughed at me like I was laughing at myself.

I had gone to the bookstore in search of inspiration, trying to find myself, scouring the aisles for ideas to write about. I am currently looking for the right path to take in my life to reach my ultimate goal of being a published writer. And instead of finding inspiration for myself in the bookstore, I found myself walking through the aisles and picking up books for my best friend and my boyfriend. If nothing else, I was being true to my character, and that in itself could be an essay. I tend to write stories that come from my experience. If I were to write the ultimate essay about myself, I'd have to include this tendency of mine to go searching for things to give the ones I love. Trying to make them happy — that's what makes me happy.

But this mission wasn't about them; it was

about me. I started in the magazine section, as usual. I looked for myself first and immediately found a magazine I wanted. This seemed to be a good start. Inside, however, I found articles for my boyfriend on his favorite band and his favorite movie and had to stop myself from buying him a copy, too. I reminded myself that this was about me. I had to focus on me.

I wandered down another aisle of magazines and immediately found a graphic-design magazine I wanted my best friend to have. I looked at the price, which was almost twenty dollars. By the time I sent it to him, it would be more than that. I put it down.

Me. Focus on me. My likes and interests, not theirs. I started off for the media section, thinking that I'd find something new for myself. Instead, I found a book on making films for my boyfriend, the film major, and a guide to film viewing that was published by one of my best friend's favorite magazines. This was not working. Finally, I decided to just go to the women's studies section. I saw a book about silencing women. The author felt we have a tendency in this society to teach women to be quiet and look nice and expect nothing more from them. I thought about it and glanced at other titles; most were about self-confidence building. And while I was offended that these were the only topics deemed necessary for women's study, I also realized what I had been doing practically since entering the store.

I am the one struggling to find what I want to do with my life at this stage. I have an ultimate goal, but I can't seem to settle on the right way to reach it. I have many options and can't bring myself to pursue any of them. Partly boredom, partly fear of failure and the unknown — I have decided not to decide right now and to just concentrate on writing. In the meantime, I'm finding all these books and magazine articles that would help my best friend and my boyfriend pursue their goals in life. I'm finding myself just as passionate in their pursuits as I am in my own. Sometimes I'm much more interested in theirs than in my own.

I looked at the book titles again and realized that I'd found myself: I'm a supporter. I love to talk about their goals and dreams, and when I see things that might help them along the way, I get excited. But when it comes to talking about what I want to do, to vocalizing my own dreams and goals and finding things that will help me, I am silent. The women's studies section of the bookstore seemed to be telling me that is my fate — a societal dictate.

I disagree. I see myself as a published writer . . . someday. But why not now? Is it the other portion of the women's studies section in me? When it comes to my best friend and my boyfriend, I have every confidence that they will become famous and achieve great things in their chosen careers. Why don't I feel the same about myself?

I left the women's studies section and went to

the music section to clear my head. Before leaving the store, I went back to the magazines and picked up two magazines for writers.

Beth says, "It's good to be nice to everyone around you, but you need to be nice to yourself, as well." Many women do so much for others, they forget to do for themselves. "Just last night, I was shopping for myself, and I kept finding things for my best friend and my boyfriend, and forgot why I was there." She laughed as she told me this, now aware of what she does. And she was able to continue shopping for herself.

The Road Home

F. R. Modall

What you don't know can hurt you — especially if what you don't know is yourself. My story is about recovering my "truth." Not that the journey has ended — because some days, I feel as far from my knowing as is possible. The difference is that today I can recognize that I don't know some things.

I can't tell you why, but at some point in time I became disconnected from my own true feelings and my heart. Maybe I was disconnected from the beginning. I don't know why it isn't as important as it used to be.

Growing up, something propelled me away from me. Like a stone rolling downhill, I picked up speed as I went. Each inch of ground covered, so much harder to stop the movement.

I didn't want bad things to happen to me; I just didn't believe good things could. If I took what was available — what someone else wanted me to take — there was less risk of rejection.

I always focused on what someone else wanted, needed, and felt. Because that way, I didn't have to face my confusion about not liking who I was and why I didn't feel I deserved good things for myself. So I focused on other people and becoming the person they wanted me to be.

When I met my first boyfriend, it was love at first sight. I was so happy. I had something he wanted! He wanted to be with me all the time. He said he loved me. I decided to become what he wanted me to be.

I struggled with the sex thing, but the truth is, I wanted so much for him to love me, there was no choice. I had the hardest time learning how to say "I love you." I didn't know how to love, but I soon learned to fake it. I learned to fake lots of things over the years.

When I got pregnant, he had to tell my parents. I probably never would have told them, not even if they'd asked. I just couldn't find my voice. My true self had long since been left behind. My boyfriend wanted to get married, so we did.

Although in many ways my pregnancy was the most difficult experience of my life, it has also turned out to be the best thing that ever happened to me. My son has been my greatest blessing.

We were divorced within the year, but not before I found what were to become my very best friends — drugs and alcohol. Finally, I could completely escape myself. I loved what they did for me! I felt like I was okay. At last, I fit in.

I became a party girl and a "free spirit." I ran with the party group. At seventeen, just prior to graduation from high school, I met my second husband. We both loved to drink. My motives for marrying this time were not even as pure as the first time. I think I just wanted to move into my own house and be away from my parents. However, I only moved from my parents' house to his house. My drinking got worse.

This marriage lasted three years. I began to question my sanity. I remember calling a hot line and telling the person on the other end of the phone that I was completely crazy. The truth is, my behavior was insane, but those few moments of clarity, when I made that call, soon vanished and didn't visit me again for many years.

I thought leaving that marriage would solve all my problems and I swore to myself that I would never depend on anyone else again! For the first time, I was doing what I wanted to do. It was true that I didn't answer to any person.

But I very quickly turned my life over to my new master. Except my "best friend" started to turn against me. It didn't make me feel good anymore. I didn't know that my value must come from within my heart. Even drunk, I couldn't capture the sense that I was all right.

During all this, I fit my son in as best I could, but alcohol and drugs came first. I no longer had a choice. My deepest regrets stem from being a bad parent. He suffered because I was a drunk. I had to have it. And because I had no idea how to love myself, I couldn't give him what he needed the most — the ability to learn how to love himself.

I began to see counselors. Drinking was causing major problems in my life. But I never mentioned this to the counselors. It was my secret, which I hid even from myself.

During the next ten years, I moved to different states, took different jobs, and met different people. Except that everywhere I went, there I was with all the same problems. Geographical changes didn't help!

And then I met the man of my dreams. I believed that at last I had found my true love. This was a man who knew what he wanted, and knew what he wanted in a woman. This was the strongest form of drug available. A place to be totally lost. The rivalry between the drink and the relationship began.

My marriage to this man was one of the most painful things to happen in my life. And when I make a list of the things for which I am most grateful, it's near the top.

After twenty years of using alcohol, through the pain of trying to be what my husband wanted me to be, I found the courage to admit to myself that I had a big problem, that I could not stop drinking, and that I needed help. With the help of a power greater than myself, Alcoholics Anonymous, and the many friends I met there, I got sober.

This was the first step toward becoming true to myself. I began a long journey back to me and the truth about myself. Who is this woman whose body I live in?

When I was a little girl, I used to look at the way the sun would make certain stones in the sidewalk shine and sparkle like little pieces of gold and diamonds. I would pretend that if I wanted to, I could chip away the cement and pull one out and I would be rich. It made me feel like anytime I wanted, all the riches of the world were right there at my feet; all I had to do was go dig them up. I loved the way this made me feel.

This is how I feel about myself today. Many years of hiding from myself, packing my feelings deep down inside, don't just disappear because I've had a change of heart and want to be different. It takes some time and a lot of work to change. I have to be patient and willing to look honestly at myself.

I'm working on forgiving myself for the wrongs I've done to my son, my family, and mostly myself. I'm learning how to say I need and deserve something better. I've given up on looking for someone to take care of me and I'm learning to take care of myself. I know that to get good at these things will take practice.

I am single again, and I am building a better relationship with my son. I want to help him begin to know his true self and understand that he deserves good things in life, too. Our progress is slow but steady.

I do not know if I will ever have that great relationship with a man. But I'm learning that all relationships are worth working on if they are worth having. I am blessed to have some wonderful friends who have helped me through some pretty rough times. I value these relationships more than I ever thought possible.

I am on the road back to me. And I am not afraid. I look forward to meeting the woman that is me.

Ms. Modall works for an organization that helps children with life-threatening illnesses. She claims that helping others has helped her to discover herself. She is learning more about herself each day, and "enjoys a close relationship with her son."

A New Lease on Life

Audrey McParlin

September of 1960 changed my life forever. I joined a convent — much to the dismay of my mother.

In a few short weeks, I found myself in a state mental hospital with the diagnosis of a breakdown and a prognosis of good. It was only much later in my life that I came to the realization that I did not have a vocation to become a sister.

I was only twenty-one, and my bipolar disorder has been my burden for all these many years. The episodes were different and the cures only temporary. At last, through the miracle of the doctor and lithium, I was given a new lease on life.

However, because I was maintained on lithium for twenty-five years, I became toxic and suffered a major setback, which baffled me and my doctors.

I always had the support of my family and friends. Although I never married, I did have a good social life in my earlier years. Now I am fifty-eight years old and, I must admit, I am thankful to be able to tell my own story — as I see it. I taught school for twenty years and I am grateful for that experience. I am retired now, and I am pleased that I am able to share my story with others!

Bipolar disorder has become a catchphrase for all types of manic-depressive illnesses. Everyone seems to be an expert in this field of psychology. Actually, it only recently came out of the closet — but I was well ahead of the pack. I had studied some psychology in college and graduate school, but I remained just another victim dependent on medication and therapy for the rest of my life.

There are so many different ways of looking at life. Success in a given vocation was what I was striving for: to be the best teacher I could be and to help my students realize their potential. However, as the years rolled on, I would have to miss one or two months of the school year while I was getting myself back together. First it would be the hospital, and then recuperation at home, and finally back to school.

I dealt with my disability as best as I could, but finally my doctors agreed that teaching was no longer for me. I was surprised at how I felt; in fact, I was relieved. I knew for some time that the stress and responsibility of teaching was beyond me now.

I began volunteer work at the county hospital and I found a new peace and meaning for my existence. Helping others always gives more to the giver than to the recipient.

After my father died, my mother and I moved to south Jersey; and after we are settled, I intend to start a new life for myself. Of course, there are still doctors and medication, but my life is filled with hope. My faith has brought me this far, and I know with continued prayers, God will help me realize my new ambitions.

Audrey's formal education was instilled by the Sisters of Charity and later by the Felician Sisters. She then attended college and began working on her master's degree after teaching for a year. She believes writing has helped her to accept her challenges and to express her feelings. "I always loved writing — particularly poetry."

Clouded by
an Obsession

Michelle Christiansen Cruz

I might as well have been on drugs. My mind was altered, clouded by an obsession with my body and food. No one could enter into the world that I secluded myself in. I thought I had complete control, but, actually, my obsessions did. They ran my life and controlled how I felt every second of the day. If I ate nothing, I felt great and powerful. If I ate something bad for me, I must be punished. Either I would have to work out extra hard or I had to purge. Then everything would be okay and back to normal for the time being. This way of life became very habit-forming and exhausting. I laughed and appeared happy on the outside, but was dying on the inside. Everything seemed to be fine, but it wasn't. I wanted to think and believe it was, but my daily battle within kept me on edge and never satisfied. When would the battle end? Who would win? I wanted to be like other girls, who weren't obsessed with their bodies and being thin. I wanted to know what it was like not to worry about what I ate or how much I weighed. I wondered what life would be like without an eating disorder. How could my weight be so powerful that it controlled my mood, feelings about my self-worth, my energy level, my motivation level, *my life!*

I thought I was going to die a bulimic. But after seven years of living with the obsession, I finally let myself realize that I wasn't happy. Only I could make the decision to change. Little did I know how hard it would be. I really fought it at first because I was scared to change. I expected to be better right away, but I didn't learn this overnight, and I surely could not expect to change overnight. I compare it with learning to walk. At first, you try to take a step, and you fall. You try again this time taking two steps, and fall. Those three steps that you did take motivate you to want to try again. The more you try, the more practice you get. That doesn't mean you don't get bruised from all your trying. You then start taking steps four, five, six, and so on. You are on your way now and standing strong on your own two feet. It is kind of shaky, but you're there and you did it. Expect to trip sometimes, but don't let that get you down. I admit sometimes when I trip and fall, I don't feel like getting up. I remain down until I choose to get up and walk again. Sometimes I even need someone to help me up. I accept help until I can stand on my own again. One foot in front of the other, I venture on.

I now see life in a different light. I began to live, feel, and experience things I had never let myself. I am alive! Friendships are real and wonderful. I felt very vulnerable and scared at first, but I had to take risks in order to get anywhere. I also feel that I have brought the focus off myself, so I have time for others. I have let people love me and I am able to show my love for others. I feel fortunate that God gave me a second chance in life.

Michelle hopes to use her new outlook on life to make a difference. "I overcame a variety of difficult experiences in my life, and I want to be able to help others through my writing." Michelle is currently working on writing a book that she hopes will accomplish this goal.

A
Time
for
Healing

A Fine Line

Marilyn Mather

I was cleaning today and came upon a brass and enamel tray that I've had for seventeen years. Seventeen years ago, that tray signified the last happy moment of my life.

I won the brass tray at a women's dinner party. That day is distinctly etched in my mind. Although I don't remember what I had for dinner, or who exactly sponsored the dinner, I remember previewing the door prizes, and my eyes locked onto a beautiful brass tray with an enamel peacock. It was different, and I like different and unusual things. I just knew that tray was mine.

I couldn't wait to go home and tell my husband of my premonition of winning the tray, and actually having it in hand. Charlie and I had been married for six years and were very happy. That night, as we made love, Charlie found a lump in my breast.

A few weeks later, while recuperating from breast surgery, I passed through my dining room and saw the peacock tray. My body surged with mixed feelings. I remembered how happy I had been that night I won it and I also remembered the instant, the exact point in time that same night, when happiness was ripped from my heart. At twenty-eight, I felt I would no longer be happy again in life. I grabbed the tray, ready to throw it out, because I knew it would be a constant reminder of the night my life was altered forever.

But I didn't throw the tray out. Nothing would change what had happened, so there would be nothing to be gained. To this day, whenever I see the peacock tray, I am reminded of the profound sadness I felt seventeen years ago and my eyes fill with tears. Over the years, I have had many happy moments, and more sad ones, too. Life is a constant push-pull of sad and happy, ups and downs. We must have the sad in order to really feel the happy.

One year and one month after my breast surgery, my daughter was born. Talk about happy! Arlene brought me a tremendous amount of joy. When Arlene was nine, I got divorced and had a mountain of financial problems. Needless to say, it was a sad time. Some days I thought the problems were insurmountable. With perseverance and a dogged desire to succeed on my own, the problems went away. New ones surface and then they fade, each time bringing a new strength.

So today when I picked up the peacock tray and remembered that fateful night when my life seemed over, I cried. Thinking of the surgery still makes me cry, but it's just one of the sad moments in my life. Life is a fine line and so delicate. It's a balance of opposites: life/death, rich/poor, healthy/sick, happy/sad. At any moment, the scale can tip either way, and you cross the line. But in life, crossing the line is usually temporary — we just don't know how long the temporary will be.

The peacock tray holds a prominent place in my home and heart because it's my reminder to relish the happy moments and endure the sad; to know that neither are permanent; and to gather strength and love through prayer and family. Here's wishing that everyone's sad moments pass quickly so there's much more time to enjoy the happy ones.

"I don't live in sadness, and it is this back-and-forth of sad/happy that inspired me to put the tray down and write this story," Marilyn says. She feels that "sparks of inspiration" can be harnessed and shared, whether through conversation, writing, or in a song. Another source of creative impulse for Marilyn is her daughter, Arlene, and her grandson, Avery.

Number Three

J. C. Summers

The spray was freezing cold. As her skin became numb enough to insert the needle into its port, Alison cringed. The needle prick didn't hurt at all, but what came after made her want to throw up already. Only nine more to go. You can do anything twelve times, right? Alison tried to remember that as the nausea medicine began to make her vision blur. Nausea medicine, what a joke. After number two, Alison had thrown up twenty-three times. It was a good thing the rug burns on her knees had healed in time to do it all again.

Inside the chemotherapy room, the eight blue recliners were filled. Alison was the luckiest. She had Hodgkin's disease, which is one of the most curable forms of cancer. Alison tried to remind herself of that as she looked around the room. So many sad and defeated faces. Defeated by the common sense and the love for those around them that forced their exhausted bodies into these chairs again and again. Living a few good years would be so much easier, but there were spouses, children, parents, siblings, and friends to consider. All of them had futures that included someone in a blue recliner. For that reason, assorted loved ones sat uncomfortably in folding metal chairs and tried to make small talk.

If only the television came in better. The three hours would pass much faster if Alison could watch the soaps. No, actually that wouldn't help at all today. Alison had watched enough TV in the last six weeks that she felt confident she could predict every 1995 Emmy Award winner. There was always some show on that portrayed the "battle," as they like to call it. To Alison, it did not seem to be an accurate description. It was more like a disruption. She lived her life in two-week spurts. As soon as she began to feel well enough to leave the house, it was time to return to the blue recliner. She tried to remember that she did feel better once the first five days had passed.

Alison looked down at the white plastic switch on the IV tube that the nurses closed when they exchanged the bags. She could stop it all with one quick movement. The nurses weren't watching. Stop the flow. Take out the needle. Walk out when no one was looking. She would walk home, pack her wig, and live a happy life for a few years. Everyone would get over it eventually. After all, it was her body, right? It used to be her body, until the doctors told her it had been confiscated for medical research.

Alison took out the new tape player her dad had bought her, and put her headphones on under the denim hat she now wore almost every day. Wearing a wig during the summer in Arizona had turned out to be a lot like walking around with a space heater on her head, so she preferred the hat. It had been very hard to buy hair. She had tried on a wig that was shaped exactly like her usual hairstyle, and it looked awful. After experimenting with every color and style in the store, she settled on a wig that was straighter and lighter than her natural hair. Apparently, she had been walking around for years with bad hair, and nobody had mentioned it.

Alison was feeling light-headed and a little nauseous. There was no way she could make it through the next five days, much less the next five months. Her hand reached down and turned off the white switch. This was definitely the right decision. She looked around to make sure no one was paying attention. Alison noticed a metal-chair daughter next to her was writing down a recipe as her blue-recliner mother spoke. A family recipe for stuffing. The daughter would have to make it at Thanksgiving this year.

Suddenly, everything in the room seemed to still. Even the IVs seemed to stop dripping as the silence registered the meaning of that recipe. As she comprehended the truth of the moment, Alison's hand restarted the IV. In that blue recliner, she discovered a spirit inside that she knew would prevail over the wigs, aching muscles, puking, and bad TV. She sat quietly as her IV finished, and then she returned home to the comfort of her metal-chair people.

Ms. Summer's story is inspired by her personal battle with Hodgkin's disease. She faces her trial with wit, seeking the beneficial aspects. "I have found that, in many ways, having cancer can be a very positive experience." Throughout the course of her treatment, she encountered patients who displayed indefatigable strength and dignity. Enduring the mental and physical challenges of cancer is an incredible strain on everyone involved. "My parents, sister, and close friends stand out as remarkable examples of supportive and loving survivors."

She is graduating with a degree in English and then will begin working on her master of fine arts degree in creative writing. She hopes her story has shed some light on the hardships, along with the rewards and humor, that can be found in this type of difficult situation.

Laughing Through
the Tears

Janice Fouks Blum

I had been treated to a pedicure at home. The phone rang beside me.

The pedicurist asked, "What's this?"

I glanced down at what had become a familiar ugly dark scab.

"I think I cut my leg shaving in the shower."

"What's up?" asked my phone friend.

"There's this weird-looking black thing on my leg."

I described it. She anxiously implored, "Go see a dermatologist immediately!"

That phone call changed my life.

The dermatologist was warm, friendly, talkative — until he saw the big black ugly scab on my leg.

"My God! This looks like a melanoma!" he screamed.

Not knowing what a melanoma was, I couldn't share in his hysterics. Sounds like an Italian dish, I thought to myself.

"We have to get a biopsy immediately. You may have cancer, a serious form of cancer."

I didn't hear anything after the word *cancer.*

My first thought was that I didn't have time for this. How absurd. Does anyone ever have time for cancer?

"What are my chances if I do have it?" I asked.

"Fifty percent," he replied.

As bad as I am at math, even I realized those weren't great odds. As the reality began to sink in, the tears started to flow. He offered me Valium. Two or three times. I really could have used some soothing words.

The diagnosis was confirmed. More offers of Valium. How about another diagnosis?

My anger was unbelievable! You ask yourself a million times, Why me? . . . Well, why not me? If it hadn't been me, it would have been some other vibrant thirty-five-year-old woman. Life's a great big lottery game, and sometimes your number just comes up.

I knew of a noted oncologist who practiced in Santa Monica, California. I packed my bags and headed south.

The doctor had a serious demeanor, but when I looked into his beautiful blue eyes, I saw a gentle soul that radiated kindness and concern.

"Do you smoke? Get exercise? . . . Any loss of appetite?"

"Not in this lifetime." I laughed.

"Is this the result of all my diet 7-Up?" I asked innocently.

"No," he vehemently replied.

He explained that melanoma was the result of having been burned extensively by the sun as a young child. It usually surfaced within young people in their late twenties or early thirties. I flashed back on a vacation with my parents to Las Vegas. I was thirteen or fourteen at the time. I sunbathed with that lethal combination of baby oil and an aluminum reflector. By the end of the day, I was burnt to a crisp. Was this medical diagnosis the result of that vacation? I'll never know.

"What are my odds?" I asked.

"We don't believe in odds. And we don't take on any losers," he responded with a twinkle. "You're young and a good personality type for survival."

In high school when a guy didn't have anything really great to say about a woman, he'd say, "She's got a great personality."

The surgical procedure was called "aggressive surgery." The tumor would be removed and they would graft skin from the right thigh in order to compensate for the loss of skin around the tumor area. All my lymph glands from my left leg and groin area would be removed. After two weeks' hospitalization, I'd be on crutches until I could walk again. They had no idea if the cancer had progressed into my lymph glands. If the lymph glands were free from cancer cells, I would have a chance at a normal life span.

The hospital became my new home. I was frightened and unsure. Thanks to Norman Cousins's theory of humor in *Anatomy of an Illness*, I decorated my hospital room with balloons and mementos from friends.

I don't remember much of the surgery or what came afterward. I was frustrated by the severity of the pain and being so damn uncomfortable. Bandages were everywhere. And so many scars. Often I joked, "Put my body against my lasagna, my lasagna would win out," but this was a bit overwhelming even for someone known for her self-deprecating humor.

The surgery was a success. The lab results indicated the lymph nodes were clear.

The tumor had been removed from my left calf, where all the essential tendons are located that we use for walking. I would have to learn to walk again. I didn't do such a great job the first time.

Thirteen years later, I often think of the many women close to my age who aren't alive — Gilda Radner, Elizabeth Glaser, women who fought a battle but didn't get the break I was given.

A cup of tea on a cold day, an hour shared with one of those afternoon talk shows, laughter with friends: More precious than diamonds are these moments of everyday life that I once took for granted.

Janice's story was inspired by a wish to share the realities of malignant melanoma. "My story reflects a desire to show the importance of humor in combating serious illness." Janice has left a career as an independent television and film producer to pursue writing. She currently lives on Martha's Vineyard and is working on her second novel.

Non Compos Mentis

Lauri Maerov

Rena and I stood silently in the elevator with the cheap brown veneer. Our uncle was across from us. He stared trying to remember who we were, knowing we were there for a reason.

We stepped out on the white concrete of the corridor. It faced an ugly redbrick chimney that rose, without meaning, through the center of the courtyard.

He unlocked the door to the tiny studio. His keys hung on a filthy string that emerged from the pockets of his stained khakis. He had forgotten why the keys were on the string, just as he had forgotten our identities.

The room was dark. Across from us, the twisted blinds were pulled almost shut against the afternoon light. Dirt from the broken pots on his balcony spilled into the room. The gray pile of the rug was trampled black with filth. A brand new vacuum cleaner stood inside the closet door, its accessories still boxed, its invoice unpaid.

Izzy walked over to the sofa bed. For months, he had not bothered to make it — to tuck the sheets under, smooth the blankets, or press the mattress inside its couch home. An inch of dust stood thick in the rough blue weave of the couch cushions. He pushed his body onto the dirty linens and stared at us again, waiting.

Rena sat on a round chair covered in a tarnished green velour like a skin of algae. I found its match, lifted the magazines piled on its cushion, deposited them on the floor, and sat.

In front of us, an avalanche of papers, pennies, books, dirty cups, and unopened mail spilled across the coffee table. Our uncle stared and waited.

"Do you know who I am?"

"No." He laughed nervously.

"I'm Lauri. I'm Margie's daughter."

"Margie — I'm Margie's daughter?" he asked.

"No, I'm Margie's daughter."

"I'm Margie's father."

"No, you're Margie's brother!" Rena and I protested together.

Then she asked, "Do you see our picture?"

Over the couch was a painting I had always hated — dark burgundy trees in front of tropical waters. It had hung in our first house in North Carolina for years. I hated it, too, because I thought he had taken it from us. In the fading half-light from the porch, I saw several warped and discolored photographs stuck in the picture frame. The same was true of the painting on the opposite wall. In Izzy's world, art existed only as a framing device for his family memorabilia.

He pointed out each person in the pictures as if instructing us in a history that didn't concern us. "This is Babie. This is Father. This is Mother. This is my sister Margie and my sister Clare. This is Lionel, and these are the children."

The last picture, taken only a few years before, was of my mother and sister and me sitting on the stairs of my aunt's house. "That's us," I pointed out. "We're the children."

Rena began to scream at him now. She stood up and gesticulated as if she were communicating with a prehistoric man. "That's Lauri! That's Rena!" She pointed her finger at herself and me for emphasis. Her voice was scratchy and desperate. "That's me. That's her."

He stared at each of us through the dark filter of his Alzheimer's and the grimy haze of the apartment.

"Can't you hear me?" Rena yelled.

He answered her quietly. "Yes, dear. You're shouting. Of course I can hear you."

I looked across the room to the sliding glass doors and wondered if I should navigate among the ruins to open the shades. The gray typewriter cover on the TV table distracted me. It was torn and ravaged by coffee spills and what looked like bird droppings. Underneath the cover sat the fat gray IBM Selectric I'd helped him purchase from my old boss when he was closing up his law office. It had been in Izzy's apartment for a year perhaps. He could never figure out how to use the correction key. He could not make the leap from manual to electric.

And I knew that beneath that cover, the same sheet of paper I had used to demonstrate would still be trapped inside.

"My name is Charles. Charlie — Isadore Charles Katz. I am a writer."

I wanted to peel it back and reveal to him who he was, remind him of the identity that was slowly leaving him and which in a matter of months or years would vanish entirely. Instead, I let him clutch my hand on my way to the door and kiss me good-bye with his harsh beard and my name on his lips like a butterfly trapped in a net, squeezed and beating its wings against certain death.

The incident in the story occurred after the police went to Lauri's uncle's apartment following a violent confrontation he had with his landlady. Lauri and her sister had tried to convince their uncle to enter a nursing home, and it was the first time he didn't recognize them. "My uncle was deteriorating from Alzheimer's but stubbornly refusing his family's help." Lauri's sister and cousin helped each other through this difficult time by sharing their ideas and sorrow about the situation.

Fade to Gray

Celeste Allen

I stand before the shuttered window, tensed for the day to begin as the fierce shriek of the gulls outside stabs through my closed eyes. I need not open the shutters. There will be no sun today, no sun tomorrow.

Wincing at the sound of Stephen thumping out of bed upstairs, I ease the coffeemaker's switch to ON. A moment later, "Good Lovin' " shatters the silence of the dawn, accompanied by Stephen's baritone, a half-note sharp, attacking all that remains of the quiet. I close my eyes again, lower bread into the toaster, and, absorbed by shadows, stand in front of the closed blinds of the kitchen door.

"Hey, babe," Stephen's voice bursts from above, "where's my — never mind."

I stiffen, praying that Eric won't cry, and shudder in relief when the baby sleeps on.

When Stephen bounds into the kitchen, buttoning his black flannel shirt, I know an hour has vanished. But I don't know where to.

"Good morning, my love." He kisses the top of my head before ramming a piece of dry toast into his mouth. "Anything you need from town?" He spews crumbs as he speaks, yanking his slicker on and reaching for another piece of toast.

Snapping my eyes closed, I flinch away from the raging yellow of the coat. It does not belong. Then I shake my head and open my eyes as I feel his fingers brush my face.

"Anything I can do?" he asks gently.

I shake my head again, unable to respond to the compassion in those eyes the color of flint.

Stephen wraps me in an embrace, and I know he is waiting, hoping for me to relax. Finally, he lets me loose, kisses my forehead. "Call me if you need anything," he says.

I hear the chug of the truck bustling off to the pier and bow my head to the hours before me.

Eric's waking cry pierces the silence, and I know that time has slipped away again, and it's near ten o'clock now. I tense for him to wail, but he doesn't. He will take a bottle. I will rock him. The motions will suffice.

Later, I climb the stairs to the widow's walk, knowing what awaits me before I even open the door leading out. Leaden sky above, and the cruel ocean tearing at angry black rocks below. Sky and sea dwindle away in the gray distance.

I cross the cardigan over my breast, open the door, and walk out. The damp salt air encrusts my face, and I blink back a tear. Salt on salt. Terns wheel overhead, fighting the wind. If I step over the rail now, I could fly with them. But then I, too, would have to fight the wind; more battle than I can bear.

I turn my face to the wind, imagine sun

stroking my cheeks. I will wait, rock Eric, smile for Stephen. Step upon step until color returns.

I turn and silently descend the stairs, the bitter taste of the ocean air still on my lips. The memory of sun behind clouds like a ray of promise.

Celeste suffers from migraines and finds them an ongoing challenge that necessitates combining all of her faculties to confront the simple tasks of her day. In her story she illustrates a migraine by turning it into the emotions she feels when she fades to gray. "Sharing this perspective with other women could help them realize they are not alone. If you have not experienced this debilitation, you do not fully understand the shades of gray that can so quickly cloud one's day."

The
Emptying
Nest

A Mother's Farewell

Suzanne Barr

I look at my desk calendar and see that I have only ten days left to live. Deciding how to spend them isn't hard. I know what I must do. I must continue on, as if no changes are anticipated. After my "death," life will continue. Babies will still be born; relationships will begin and end; wars will be fought, won, and lost; yet, my life as I know it will no longer be.

You see, I'm not actually going to die in the sense we know it. A part of me is dying, and I painfully await its burial.

From swollen stomach to swollen feet, I eagerly await the beginning that these sometimes-unwanted changes cause.

The beginning began! Armed with advice, ideas, things to do and not to do, I coasted through the calm waters of motherhood.

Occasionally, a wave knocks around in our peaceful drift. Torrential rains with hurricane forces throw us to the shores of reality. As always, we return safely to our ship. Passages are smooth — again.

I breathe a sigh of relief . . . however temporary. I am sustained until the next gale force blows our peaceful island into rough waters. I faithfully secure my life jacket and that of my daughter. I ask my higher power to guide me to dry land.

I see an island in sight, knowing it is only a temporary haven. I sail within its boundaries, content to remain until the next storm.

Many storms rage against my shifting island. Clouds of darkness descend, clouding the brightness of times past. I fight back; my survival instinct is strong. My weapons — love, kindness, and wisdom — are armors against the winds of change. The storms are stronger, more violent. Islands clash and I continue to arm myself with patience, generosity, understanding, and humor.

Now, only an occasional tropical storm brews, leaving in its wake torn limbs, scattered roots up-lifted, lives in disarray. Careful mending, re-planting, and calm reassurance provide a new haven for the future.

Gusts of wind blow through our lives daily now. An unexpected thunderstorm reacquaints us. Reassured, we sail to bigger islands. On this new island, we find ourselves stranded, yet we are content to remain.

Sailing is smooth. A new experience binds us closer, close as the grains of sand that blanket our island. We luxuriate in their warmth and fa-miliarity. Our island is storm-free, only a random wind gust to visit us.

Biological changes begin to separate us. A fis-sure in my island — the smaller half sails away. Bit by bit, I can still see this piece of island, yet each day, new and stronger winds cause it to glide farther from view.

The days pass. Clouds of discontent homestead on my island. Its sunny waters are murky with uncertainty and loss. Hurricane winds greet me at every sunrise and torment me at each sunset.

One day, I see a trickle of sunlight filtering through the clouds of despair that cover my island. A glimmer of hope spurs me to rise above the bleak waters of uncertainty. I ask myself, Could it be possible my lost island isn't really lost? Only drifting in another direction?

The divide between the islands remains, yet the connection is still there, reinforced by honesty, integrity, and, most of all, love. I can see the waves splashing against my little island. She is ready to venture into new seas, undiscovered. I can no longer hold her with life jackets or safety nets.

The winds blow her island farther away. I lift a hand in passing, saluting the captain. For that she is. Her island, her ship, and I must relinquish my command. I'll content myself with being first mate.

Smiling, I wave one last time as my small island calmly sails away.

A high-sea adventure awaits her. But, I will be her anchor. I will be a temporary port for my smallest island.

Farewell, little one. May your waters be calm and your sailing exceed that of those before you.

I am here, always, your safety net in the sea of life.

Mother

Suzanne wrote her story for her daughter, who was moving across the country. "Saddened that she was leaving, I wanted to give her something to explain how I felt." Suzanne and her daughter are extremely close, and the day her daughter left was "the saddest day of my life." She told me she cried on her sister's shoulder and her husband's. She also had a lot of friends going through the same passage, and they supported and comforted one another. "You have to let go, and trust in what you've taught your child." This is motherhood's most bittersweet lesson.

Go West, Young Man

Terri Watrous Berry

Well, it has finally hit me. My husband says that he has been wondering when it would.

My eldest child — my twenty-three-year-old son — is moving away. Far away. Across time lines away.

The U-Haul has been reserved. He will pick it up to pack next Sunday. His preparing to leave has actually turned into his leaving; it is not just an abstract plan anymore. The future, it appears, is now.

And it is my own words that are echoing loudest in my ears; "Go for it," I said. Go for it. *Go* — for it seems that youthful futures do dissolve, surprisingly fast, into pasts. And the desire to sow oneself into distant fields fades as surely as good eyesight and the memory of limber limbs. Young roots, certainly, are the most successfully replanted. But something else is going with him when he leaves, for this is the end of an era for me. An era that began when I married his father, and my son was only a plan for a future I'd yet to meet.

Once he arrived, we plowed forward together, through all the additions to and subtractions from our family. A family that, like all others, grew and grieved, mended and moved on, burying hatchets and dogs and grandparents. Together, he and I welcomed his brother and sister and, eventually, even a new dad, when we had to let his own daddy go to where *his* dreams led.

My firstborn. The one whom I made my new-mother mistakes on; the one who seemed to be raising me as I was trying to figure out how to raise him. Through all the other changes, he was there. Through his brother's and sister's teenage trials and tribulations, he was there — with me, beside me, supporting me.

Obviously, he is more than just my son. Because of his own open, principled, insightful, and understanding ways, he became — and remains — my friend. I am only now starting to realize just how much I'm going to miss him.

And his leaving really does usher in the beginning of the end of life as I have lived and loved it these past twenty-odd years. Someday, when the others have also grown and gone, this most important portion of my life will be but a memory, growing ever more distant as the years pass. As intangible, except in my heart, as the family in which I grew up has become.

I am thinking now how blind I was to my own mother's sense of loss when I first married and moved away. And about how she only let me see her joy for me on that long-ago good-bye day when I left to pursue my dream. Me, the last of her children to marry; her, being left quite alone in our family home, as my father had already passed on.

My marriage was ending an era for her, yet I gave scant thought or recognition to that then. Of course, at twenty, I was ill-equipped to understand it; unable to see it from any perspective but my own. Life to me then was all future, when so much of life, for her, was already past.

She used to tell me that I would look at many things differently when I got older, and I, in my youthful ignorance, staunchly argued otherwise. I had all of the answers then; why should they change as I aged?

Oh, but they do. Because the questions change. What is really important? What is not? How do you know the difference? How do you hang on? How do you let go? How indeed. With grace, with style, and with a smile. Just like my mother did. This is not a lesson I was expecting to be learning — at this late date — from her.

You did good, Mom. That day that I hugged you and hopped happily into the loaded-down little yellow '67 Mustang and pulled away from your curb, with my brand-new husband, you did good. For it is only now — twenty-five years later — when faced with watching my own child heading off into the horizon, that I wonder, for the first time, what my own mother did after we drove away.

My eyes, you see, were on a sunrise. Little did I understand that hers were on the waning light of her best and brightest days. And if I had looked back, even once, I might have been able to see my own rainbow, refracted through the shining of her tears.

"The passage that mothers must navigate when a child moves away holds some dark twists and turns, but it is the child's own glowing dreams that help illuminate our way through," says Terri. Life is unpredictable, and after her struggle to deal with her son's departure, her son not only returned but also temporarily lived in his old room. Terri notes, "Be careful what you wish for; apparently, labors of love are never quite finished when we think they are."

Happiness Is When the Kids Are Grown

Janice Tatum

Remember when your children were young and you tucked them into bed at night, all soft and cozy in their jammies and smelling of soap? And later when you locked the doors and turned out all the lights to go to bed yourself, the warm feeling of having your family safe and snug in their beds? It is hard to imagine that someday they will be out on their own and living under another roof. And that you will be able to handle that emotionally.

But when the teen years arrive, you begin to wonder if that day of independence will ever come. I truly believe God plans for teenagers to behave in such an obnoxious manner to help parents look forward to the time when that awful noise they call "music" will no longer be played, and when they will finally discover that perhaps they don't know *everything* after all.

Then, one morning, you wake up and discover that the huge job of raising your children is behind you. They are adults now. You look at your husband across the breakfast table and you wonder, Who is this person? Do I still love him?

Do I even know him?

For so many years, while our lives are filled with school activities and molding little people into responsible adults, we sometimes lose touch of why we married each other all those years ago. Now it's time for rediscovery, and a time to take the romance out of the closet! Dust it off and rejuvenate it with a more mature flavor than in the years before you started your family. You already know his habits; you know where he squeezes the toothpaste tube and that he leaves the toilet seat up. But you may not have noticed that his temples are graying. And don't you think it looks distinguished?

It is now time to create a new life together. Many people forget to do this and let the "empty nest" syndrome take hold of them, or, worse yet, stay so involved in their children's lives that they are unable to try their new wings of independence. That is almost like telling them you think they are not able to take care of themselves and you must still help them.

If you spend too much time with these fresh new adults after they leave home, it is too easy to tell them when you see them traveling down the wrong road and headed for trouble. Which, of course, will only be met with disgust and comments about how much smarter they are than you. And how you can't possibly understand — you're too old.

So instead, go to the phone and make dinner reservations at the most romantic restaurant in town. Then go to your closet and select your most attractive dress; paint your nails and have your hair done. Now you are ready for your most important date!

Over dinner and a bottle of wine, you can discuss many things you never had time to talk about before. You may want to plan a romantic vacation alone, or take up golf and join a local golf club. You will likely discover that this man you share your life with really is quite a guy, and now you remember why you married him. A new era has begun!

Janice now has time to pursue a longtime dream of writing. "I have a number of ideas I would like to write about, so I decided to take a writing course to feel better prepared to reach my goal." She also entered new and unfamiliar territory, acting as the general contractor when she and her husband built a house. It was a rewarding experience, and a "story in itself."

Reflections on Becoming the Mother of a Wife

Diana Anhalt

Last year for a few glorious months, I was mother of the bride. During the weeks that preceded, caught up in the frenzy of activities accompanying a wedding, my daughter Sarah and I — always close — grew even closer. We talked nonstop and reminisced about things we hadn't discussed in years.

"Do you remember," I asked, "how thrilled you were to take fourth place in the kindergarten swimming contest?"

"Boy, do I ever, and there were only four competitors. I think I still have the medal!" We giggled and walked down the street holding hands. "Or when I was driving myself to school for the first time and the earthquake hit? I thought the telephone poles were shaking and the car was weaving back and forth because I'd turned the steering wheel in the wrong direction."

Although we hadn't lived in the same part of the country for over twenty years, when we did see each other every few months, our moments

202

together were intense and immensely satisfying. Prior to the wedding, I flew cross-country to help her choose her wedding dress. She had made an appointment at a bridal store in Brooklyn six weeks earlier, and I arranged to meet her at the subway station. Then, without the slightest justification, I simply lost track of the time, arriving almost an hour late. "How could you forget?" she kept asking me. "You come all the way to New York and you forget? Don't you want me to get married?"

Perhaps, at some level, I didn't. It had never occurred to me before the wedding — although I wish it had — that the moment she moved down the aisle on the arm of her husband, my role as confidante, best friend, adviser, and ally would end. Realization dawned slowly as telephone messages went unanswered, invitations were canceled at the last moment, and previously ordinary subjects of conversation became taboo.

Our long-distance telephone conversations, formerly filled with hoots of laughter, nonstop chatter, and a sense of intimacy, dwindled from forty minutes to ten, and she sounded anxious to get on to something else. "Have I done something wrong?" I'd ask.

"No, of course not, Mom. You always blame yourself for things that haven't happened."

Despite my extraordinary capacity for denial, at some point I was forced to accept that not only was I no longer number one in her life, and probably hadn't been for at least twenty years, but I was being patently unfair to her and my son-in-law — no matter how keen my own sense of loss. She did what I had done by making room for her husband by her side. From here on in, he would come first; a commitment is an all-or-nothing thing.

I remembered how, shortly after my own marriage, my parents called to ask if they could come stay with us for a few days. The look on my husband's face when I mentioned their plans was enough to make me pick up the phone and lie into the receiver: "We'd really love to have you, but the sofa bed is broken. Next time, okay?" They knew better than to ask ever again, and now I sometimes wonder if my mother felt the same emptiness I did, that dull ache below the rib cage.

Over the years, my parents and my husband and I drew together more closely, learning to lean on one another, as friends. I never fully confided in them again, and as we modified our expectations, the nature of the relationship turned less competitive, less emotionally charged. My mother and I were wives together and, then, mothers. The bonds between us tightened, but they were never the same. The same thing will happen in our relationship with Sarah and our son-in-law. As time passes, we will surely cross back toward one another, bridging the gaps. At least now I realize why I reacted the way I did: because when I least expected it, the hard ground beneath me shifted, leaving me unprepared for the upheaval, which, like an earth-quake, was silent and left marks.

"I had every reason to be content, and I thought I was. My only daughter married a wonderful man; my husband retired, and we were spending more time together; my research on American po-litical exiles in Mexico was going well, and I had sold a few articles," says Diana. She didn't realize until after she wrote this story how and, more im-portantly, why things were no longer the same. "Of course I am still a mother and wife, but my life has changed without warning, and — worse yet — without my permission."

My Second Chance for Happiness

Winifred Pichardo

Looking back over the past years of my life, I have begun to wonder what I have accomplished of any importance and value, and what I have achieved. In what way has my being here influenced and/or benefited those around me — especially those dear to my heart?

As far back as I can remember, I was always extremely maternal. I was seven years old when my first brother was born, followed two years later by the birth of my second brother. Indeed, I was their sister; however, I cared for and loved them as though I were their mother. Of course, being just kids, we all played games and had fun and silly times, but I always felt protective and responsible toward them. Even though we were seven and nine years apart, respectively, I practically brought up my brothers, and for all purposes, they were my sons. I even took care of my sister (two years my senior) and helped her in any way I could.

During my school years and later while at the workplace, I found that away from home, I worried about my brothers' safety and well-being.

To this day, my brothers stress the fact that my love, caring, and guidance had an impact on their lives in very beneficial ways.

I eventually went on to marry, and I became the mother of two daughters. I loved being a mom and I know that I devoted 100 percent of myself to raising my children. As normally happens, my daughters grew up, completed their education, and married.

I felt sad and incomplete, and sometimes lost. I realize it was not because they moved on in their lives, but actually because I had no one to take care of and nurture any longer. I did not feel whole or fulfilled. Having my own share of problems, things looked bleak for a chance of happiness in my life. So I went to work every day, cooked, cleaned, laundered, visited, pursued hobbies, and functioned, but something was definitely missing from my life and my heart. My life was to change dramatically when one day my daughter announced her pregnancy. At first, I did not feel anything one way or the other, and I could not begin to imagine how I would feel being a grandmother. On that eventful day when my first grandchild was born, I was given a second chance at happiness — happiness wrapped up in a pure, innocent, precious gift of love.

Now that I am a grandmother of four, I realize my purpose on earth — to be a loving mother and grandmother in every aspect of these honorable times of life. It all fits together like perfectly matched patches in the quilt of life.

Nothing makes me happier than to see my grandchildren growing and progressing and responding to what I teach them with eagerness and love. We have learning times together, and, best of all, fun times, when they transport me, heart and soul, to that innocent, youthful world of theirs, filled with wonder, curiosity, and hope.

I may not be a professional success or wealthy or famous, but we all have our own calling in life. I always was a very maternal woman, and at this time in my life, I have found a comforting, rewarding, heartwarming reason to be — I am a grandmother!

After having taken stock of my life, the lessons to be learned have become very apparent. I have conducted my life as I have because I am me. There is no sense in fretting over the what ifs, the what could have beens, or what is to be. The idea is to take each day as it comes and to try to enjoy it with positive feelings, and to appreciate what we do have.

In this modern, cold, overly technical, programmed world of ours, nothing can ever rise above or take the place of plain old-fashioned caring, love, and the human touch. No matter how we are forced, by today's standards, to achieve higher positions and riches, the most important and precious parts and functions of our lives are free. For me, the innocent twinkle in a small child's eye and the unconditional love that these "tiny people," my grandchildren, so unselfishly lavish upon me is worth more than any treasure on earth.

Winifred has four grandchildren, three grandsons, and a new granddaughter. "They are my special treasures and my inspiration. They help me through the difficult times and renew my spirit, but, it's my first grandson who changed my life most dramatically." Winifred writes a "Grandma's Corner" column for her local newspaper.

Forever Young

Beckie A. Miller

Children have managed to drive me crazy and keep me sane at the same time — they have made me laugh, cry, scream, and shout. I guess that is why, at this late time in my life, I am choosing to be a parent all over again, by adopting a new little girl. She joins the ranks as little sister to our now oldest daughter, and she helps fill a void left by the death of our son. He was a great brother to Christie, and I am sure he looks down upon our newest, Kimberlie, and guards her from harm.

I had a well-meaning person tell me, when he learned of the pending birth of this baby we were going to adopt, that I could not replace my son with this infant. Of course we can never replace our son — but that does not mean that we do not have room in our hearts to love another child or that her place in our lives cannot fill some of the emptiness we feel. I have loved many kids over the years, my own, and those I've known through my eighteen years of providing home day care, and every time one grows up and moves on, a piece of me is lost. That is the hardest part of child care. Yet I do it again and again, knowing full well the rewards outweigh the pain.

A few years ago, one of my toddlers, who was

four years old at the time, made me laugh despite the seriousness of what she was saying. She had been, along with the rest of my family, attempting to deal with our son Brian's death. On a family trip up to the mountains, she explained to her mom that within the crescent moon, in the sky overhead, was Brian's leg dangling out of heaven.

Oftentimes, the simplicity of what children believe is just as uncomplicated as life really should be. When our pet rooster died, the kids told me not to cry, for now Brian has someone in heaven to play with. If all of us could look at life through children's eyes, no matter what age we become, we could face anything life threw at us. Whether it were tragedy and painful loss, or disability of some kind, a child's-eye view could show us the truth in any situation.

Friends and strangers often tell me how young I look for my age. The truth is, being a part of so many children's lives has kept me this way. It is simply not true that children cause gray hair and wrinkles — though teenagers may qualify in this respect! I did not have much of a childhood myself, and I have been lucky enough to have relived what I missed many times over.

When our son was killed — and there is no gentle or humorous way to ease into this, he was robbed and shot to death shortly after his eighteenth birthday — I resumed caring for the children in my day-care center only five days after his funeral. While I was in deep emotional pain, I also knew instinctively that the children would help me endure the incredible pain of the loss of my son.

It was a journey we took together. Sometimes they stopped me cold with their frank questions about the men who killed Brian. Yet we talked and cried, laughed and hugged our way through something no one should ever have to endure. I was and am, though they are now all older and in school, closer to that group of my little ones than any other. They do not let my son's memory die, and they are forever touched by the horror of his death, but in ways that I hope will one day allow them to grow up and change this world with their compassion.

Now, as I begin another phase in my life as a renewed mother, I am reminded, continuously of how much children have brought and bring to my life. I truly never thought, once my son was killed, that I would ever experience absolute joy again. Little did I know that years after his death, through the magic of healing, and through the help of all the children in my life, I would make room in my heart and risk the chance of loss by giving my heart completely to another child. Kimberlie has opened a new world, not only for me but for her older sister and her doting dad, my husband, Don. Christie has become a big sister and is no longer left an only child — something she hated as much as the pain of losing her brother. Don has a new little daughter, whom he teases, and who will grow up and work on cars with him and play basketball. Who knows what she will eventually do, but she will do it with much love. And through this child of ours, a most precious gift of love, our hearts, once darkened by incredible loss, will be forever young.

Beckie is a housewife, mother, and day-care provider. She is the leader of the Phoenix chapter of Parents of Murdered Children, a support group for family and friends of homicide victims. "All the children in my life gave me the motivation to survive. They eased my journey through a horror no one should ever have to endure." Sharing her story has been an important part of her healing, yet she'll never truly recover from the tragedy. In dealing with the question of "why?" she realized, "It will always be difficult . . . but you make the choice to go on, and find the goodness in life."

Follow
Your
Dream

Backseat Syndrome

P. J. Hill

I have been married for over two decades and my children are now in college. It's my turn. It's my turn to do whatever it is that I want to do. I can finally get into the driver's seat. The problem is that even though it is my turn, I have no idea what I want to do. I have taken a backseat to life, and now I don't remember how to drive. I'm not alone.

Three of my friends confided in me that their marriage problems really escalated when their children left home. One is divorced, and two are hanging on by a thread. As I listened to my friends, I began to hear a pattern. Our husbands surmised that either the "empty nest" syndrome or the onset of menopause was the culprit. They theorized that we would adjust in time. After all, their lives really haven't changed. They get up, go to work, come home, have dinner, and immerse themselves in their passion — whatever that passion may be.

We, on the other hand, notice a big change. While the onset of menopause may explain the mood swings and the "empty nest" syndrome may be the label used for not feeling needed, there is another element that is obstructing our happiness. I call it "the backseat syndrome." That disquieting underlying feeling has a name.

Taking a backseat has been almost inbred in women. Our fathers were the drivers in our houses when we were growing up. Our husbands are the drivers in our houses now. As children, we thought the world centered around us. Of course our moms would drive us here and pick us up there. Mom would help with the homework, and so on. Mom was there, on call whenever we needed her. Our dads spent time with us, too. Sometimes we were allowed to go with our dads when they indulged in their hobbies. But mom was always there for you when you needed her. Your children felt the same way. As moms, we were there to check the English report, make the boo-boo better, et cetera. Call our name and we were there.

While our children were growing up, we moms relished their development. Proud we were, and rightfully so. And while we were keeping the home fires burning, our husbands built careers and developed friends and activities outside the home. We thought we had it all, but one thing was missing — our dreams were missing.

Unfortunately, while our husbands and children were growing and developing, we took a backseat and suppressed our dreams and aspirations. Who had time for dreams? Our time was taken up with other obligations. We thought we would expand on our dreams later. Well, later is here, and while it's easy to say I'll do this and that, in actuality it's very difficult. Having it be our turn is a new concept for us. If we try to reach to our husbands for entertainment and companionship, we're going to fail, because our husbands are not experiencing the same life change. They will later, when they retire, but not now. The change must come from within. We must get into the driver's seat. It's our turn. It's our turn to develop and grow. Take that painting class. Go back to college. Dream your dream and make that dream a reality. Praise yourself for a job well done. Drive.

Learning about the backseat syndrome is the first step toward growing and developing. Knowing that you are not alone in your feelings eliminates the "What is wrong with me?" question. The only thing wrong is that over the years we have neglected our own wants and needs. We felt selfish if we entertained thoughts about our dreams and aspirations. We allowed our families to dictate our place in life. We allowed ourselves to believe that our husbands' and our children's needs, wants, and desires came first. Our needs, wants, and desires would be taken care of later. We took a backseat to life.

It's now our turn to drive. Take short trips to begin your journey. Do something that you have been putting off. Take time for yourself. I allow myself time to be by myself, with classical music in the background, planning what I want to do with my turn. This is a big step, because I will not allow interference from the outside. This is my time and the DO NOT DISTURB sign is prominently displayed. I dream and search within myself. I toss ideas around, reject some, and plan the implementation of others. I am discovering hidden talents and interests that I have suppressed for far too long. I am experiencing the joy of watching myself grow and develop. I applaud myself. It's my turn and I will become the driver.

When Pamela's last child left for college, she missed the everyday hubbub of family life, yet she felt it was time for a new beginning. "One stage was ending, but a new stage was dawning. It was now a time for me, but I was overshadowed by my roles as daughter, wife, and mother. Thus, this disquieting feeling became the backseat syndrome."

When suffering from this syndrome, her advice is to delve into your inner self and discover who you truly are by getting in the driver's seat. Since Pamela wrote this story, she has returned to college for a master's degree, has taken a job, and is working on a book. "Not only am I driving; I've got the pedal to the metal!"

On the Inside

Julia C. Mosteller

She had always wanted to be a writer. What had happened to her life? The ambitions held as a young child had all but faded. Her husband thought her ideas stupid. Her children treated her like the child. In her own mind, she kept a score for each time one of them spoke or treated her in a way that was designed to make her feel small. She called them "idiot points," and most days the score was high.

She watched a lot of television, mostly talk shows, flicking from station to station in an effort to find someone whose life was more pathetic than hers. She read magazines, dreamed of winning one of the competitions they ran. A forty-inch color TV, a cruise to a faraway island, the big cash prize — anything to make her feel worthwhile. Music was important to her, the radio playing songs and melodies that reminded her of a better time in her life, when she was young, attractive, and carefree. Her particular favorites taking her back to a time or place in her youth, evoking pleasant memories. Identifying with the lyrics was something she held dear.

She had worked once, owned her own home, managed her own finances. Nowadays, she just existed. Her body was running to fat. Gray hairs were showing and her feeling was that she had earned every one. Why was it that in her mind she felt as she had at sixteen or seventeen years of age? Would she feel like that as she got older, a young girl trapped in an old woman's body? In a way she hoped it would be like that, but in other ways she wished it would not.

Why had she not made wiser choices for herself? Done more with her life? How had she come to this? She was not really unhappy. Her husband was a decent man; he just failed to understand her discontent. Lots of times, she could not understand it herself. The best way to describe the feelings she had was as the breaking of her spirit, made worse by the daily soliloquy to her soul.

Escape is impossible. How she longs to settle into the roles that have been handed to her, wife, mother, homemaker, chief cook, and bottle washer! But the young girl inside her will not become resigned. Her refusal is what keeps her alive.

One day, Julia was talking to two female family members. She was expressing the same feelings illustrated in her story. Gratefully, she discovered she wasn't alone — others felt the same, irrespective of age. Born in London in 1955, she's had a full life. In 1991, she married a man she met while in Majorca, Spain. Her life changed dramatically. Moving to the United States, she be-

came a full-time mother to two stepchildren, and a housewife. "My story was prompted by genuine feelings, not regrets! For twenty-one years before my marriage I had a career. I traveled whenever I could, and my life was, on the whole, a full and independent existence. I gave it up of my own accord. I'm happy, but sometimes when all the days of the week seem the same, you feel like life is passing you by." Although Julia does not regret her choice, occasionally she wonders, What happened to me, myself, and I?

He Was Patient

Debi Sanders

Most people will agree, thirty is that horrible age in life that most people dread and fear. Thirty came and flew by like a beautiful butterfly. I was thrilled by my coming of age, at my maturity and my sophistication. I was officially one of the grown-ups.

Approaching my thirty-fifth birthday was a whole different story. I definitely had too much time on my hands, and started to reflect negatively on my life and what I'd made of it. I had always maintained part-time jobs, usually working around my two sons' schedules. I loved being with them. They were my life. I can't ever remember a time when I had another ambition other than being Mommy. We did mom-and-tot activities. School started and I went to school with them. I was the mother who headed PTOs and became room mother. I also volunteered to be den mother and team mother. I learned every sport right along with them. Reaching middle and high school, it was no longer cool for Mom to be around, so I pursued mindless part-time jobs to ensure my being home before they were. I could feel them slipping away.

I remember calling my husband at work and

asking him, "What should I do?" He was patient, very patient.

It was around this time I started noticing my gray hairs, and hair growing from my chin. Yikes, I couldn't believe I was now plucking my chinny-chin-chin. Those character lines around my eyes were much more pronounced and those laugh lines encircling my mouth were prominent. My waistline had thickened, too.

This was my becoming of age, and I didn't like it. I was scared. I looked around and could see that all my friends seemed happy. They were married, they had children, and they all worked at something they loved. They did it all. Even my mother had a successful career. They always had new ideas and were striving for new goals. Goals — I had none. My whole life revolved around my children's goals.

I called my husband and asked him, "What do I do now?" He was patient, very patient. I was desperate. I had to find new life for myself. You can only clean a house, go shopping, meet for lunch for so long, and eventually it gets boring. My only conversations regarded my boys and their antics. Or their accomplishments, their dreams, and their goals.

One morning with nothing to do, I was drinking my fourth cup of coffee and reading the newspaper, and one of the ads caught my eye. "Be a model." Yeah right! But I read on. It stated that the majority of people in the world are not like the skinny young models in magazine advertisements. Finally! This ad stated they were looking for mature women, over thirty-five years of age who were size twelve or larger. I read the ad a couple of times before I had the nerve to call the number. I actually made an appointment for the following Wednesday. I was nervous, and scared. Do I dare dream or hope? I didn't tell a soul. It was going to be my secret.

Over the next few days, I had my hair colored and cut and had a beautiful set of nails applied. I bought a new suit for my interview. I was inspired. I had a goal. I really didn't think about the job. I was thinking that, yes, I was a woman, over thirty-five, a size fourteen (okay, sixteen), and I thought that I could achieve anything. I hoped. Wednesday morning came, and I called my husband. I told him I couldn't tell him what I was about to do. He was patient, very patient.

I timidly went to my interview. They loved me. They loved my appearance, my stylish suit and my hair. I couldn't believe it was me who was actually strutting myself around their offices, selling them on me. They had a job for me, and it started two weeks later. It was an informal fashion show and I would be wearing a famous designer label at one of the better stores in the local shopping mall. They hoped I would be able to go to their workshop the next weekend, for I needed "a little polish," they said. I met the other women I'd be working with, and I picked out the wardrobe changes I'd be modeling.

I continue to enjoy informal modeling. I have

spread my wings to include informal modeling at local restaurants. I've gained great confidence and wisdom over these past five years. I am no longer just Ryan's or Steven's mom. I write. I am beautiful. I'm now approaching my fortieth birthday, and I look forward to a grand celebration!

Children give a mother a sense of self, and when they move on, it can create an undeniable void. Debi's story exemplifies the searching for new dreams and identity. Her perseverance, her husband's patience, and her two boys helped rebuild her sense of purpose and her confidence.

There Are No Shadows in the Dark

Karen Braynard

She woke up that morning with the familiar loathing for everything. She didn't want to open her eyes. She knew exactly what she'd see and didn't think she had the internal fortitude to face it head-on, not yet. She'd been waking up feeling this way for the last seven or eight months, but once she'd open her eyes, the realities that she dwelled on in her dreams would hide themselves in the dark parts of her mind, pretending not to exist during the day.

Slowly, she rubbed the hardened grains of sleep from her eyes. The orange-red lights from the digital clock indicated that it was 4:26 A.M., too early to get out of bed. But perhaps the early-morning hours are the best time to deal with the realities. After all, she thought to herself, there are no shadows in the dark. She didn't believe it and reached for the lamp. As the intense light flooded the room, she closed her eyes. She was certain that today, even with the light on, she'd see things differently, and once she opened her eyes, she could never go back to her reality.

With a surge of resolution, she opened her eyes

again, resigning herself to the uneasiness and anxiety that was sure to rush at her. But all she saw was the same room she woke up to every morning. She pushed aside the light blanket and pulled herself up from the bed. Walking barefoot across the hardwood floor, she took her robe from the chair. She had to sit down to pick off the grime embedded on the soles of her feet. She wondered when she had last swept the floors.

With great effort, she pulled on her robe and made her way to the kitchen. As she passed his room, she could hear her fourth husband's snoring over the muted voices from the television. Even with the door shut, she pictured him accurately. His strong body sprawled across the bed facedown, shirt off and jeans still on. One arm flung across the bed, the other outstretched toward the television, remote still in hand. Beside him, on the bed, lay an ashtray he'd taken home one night from the bar up the street — now filled with three or four cigarette butts properly snuffed, their fetid ends crushed. One butt still resting on the edge of the ashtray, a long ghost trail of ashes leading up to it. A couple of empty beer cans tossed onto the nightstand, along with a crumpled pack of cigarettes. The contents of his pockets carelessly heaped — a few dollars and some change, the crumpled phone number of a potential customer, whom he'd never call, and a pack of matches.

Once in the kitchen, she turned on the overhead light. The first thing to catch her eye was the painting. More than twenty years ago, she had painted this simple picture of a young girl with long brown braids playing an oversized guitar — a portrait of her own hopes and dreams. But she had allowed time to confine her creativity and shelve her hopes. She had buried her dreams and refused to look honestly into the reality she had inadvertently created for herself. Twenty years ago, she had never thought to look past her future, never realized that her choices would abandon her in this obscure darkness.

She slowly glanced around and saw what she had become. The glare from the overhead light unfurled additional proof of her self-neglect. The once-white curtains were now a dingy aged gray. The wallpaper had yellowed, separating itself from the wall. Cobwebs along the ceiling were full, having collected for almost a year. A splintered hole in the door gaped at her, testimony of an event she couldn't remember. She grabbed the back of a chair, knuckles whitening as she felt the panic engulf her. Like her home, she had become a shell, in which she cowered, desperately avoiding the reality of her life.

She tried hard to face the question that had been pushing to the surface for months. Yes, she nodded to herself. I am here, somewhere, and I must come out and live again. With a weary sigh, she put on a pot of strong coffee. As the coffee brewed, she looked out the window into her backyard. Beyond the trees, the sky was changing. Magenta and light blue swirled in magnificence. Yes, she nodded to herself again. I have much work to do. A weak yet hopeful smile lit up her face as the early-morning sun began to fill the room.

Karen says, "There can be a new beginning, but not without first facing the fear and truths we have so easily pushed into the dark areas of our minds." She feels her story is a composite of many women she's known who have faced their own future and found the energy to change the course of their lives.

She found her strength, and changed her career and lifestyle for her most treasured passions, her family and her writing. Karen lives in Germany with her "soul mate" husband and their two children.

Leap and the Net Will Appear

Paula Silverberg

Thirty years ago, it was a piece by Beethoven that did me in. Once I started playing, all I could remember was page one. Over and over again, page one, hoping no one would notice. I closed the keyboard cover after that recital and vowed it was my last. It was 1966 and I was seventeen years old. I knew I was tired of practicing, tired of performing, and certainly sick and tired of a dictatorial teacher who didn't know how to bring fun into music. Walking away from the piano after that humiliating performance was a huge relief. Staying away became easy. And stay away I did, for eleven years.

It was 1977. I was five months pregnant with my second child. I decided I wanted to play the piano again. I don't know if it was the expectation of working with my childhood teacher, the long car ride to her house, or the fact that sitting on a hard piano bench was distracting. It all ended before it really began, and then I got caught up in the life of a young mother. I didn't think about finding the time to take lessons again for another nineteen years.

It was January of 1996. The kids were out of the house and on their own. I decided to read the book *The Artist's Way* by creativity guru Julia Cameron. Before I even opened it, though, I had already taken the first step. I had made the resolution in my heart. I was going to play the piano again.

The first hurdle was to find a teacher. Effortlessly, I connected with one, and in no time at all I was reading music again. Within months, my fingers mastered a Chopin mazurka, and with that one accomplishment, I turned a corner. I could see myself as that petite ten-year-old. I'm in my elementary school auditorium. A teacher is changing the reel on some movie and I am filling the time again by performing on the piano. I am sliding up and down the bench as I joyfully play some huge concerto. God how I loved to play for people. What a memory!

I wanted to relive it as a forty-seven-year-old. Unfortunately, I was surprised to find I still had plenty of performance panic left over from my last public recital at the age of seventeen. Hell — I'll just play for myself. I don't have to play for anybody else, I thought. Would that thinking get me in front of an audience? Never. I just had to believe I could get through the heart pounding and the shaky hands and the anxiety — and the memory of that last, awful recital.

My teacher had performance evenings for just her students. Playing in front of a bunch of little kids seemed a safe way to begin again. Okay,

Julia Cameron — I am signing up to take the "leap." Let's just hope that the net will appear!

It was the day of my performance. Was I thinking about my pieces? No — I was thinking about what to wear! The audiotape on performance anxiety said "dress comfortably." It was not enough to worry about playing; now I had to think about clothing — no tight waist, no unfamiliar shoes, no long sleeves. It all made sense, but it made me a little crazy as I discarded item after item.

Driving to my teacher's house, I pictured myself at the keyboard. I pictured an audience. I tried to stay on the road. I watched as the other students arrived. They were all girls — ages nine to seventeen. They looked at the only other adult in the room besides their teacher, and I could imagine them wondering, Who is that? They got their answer when I volunteered to play first.

I cruised through my warm-up piece. Yes! I was thinking. I can do this! Then came the Chopin mazurka with its several repeated sections. It was as if I were outside of my body. I started to feel nervous. My concentration wavered. I made some mistakes, but I willed myself to play through them. Then it was over. In a matter of minutes, thirty years of performance anxiety were washed away. I was grinning from ear to ear as I bowed to my audience of children. The applause couldn't have sounded better, even if it had been a public performance at Carnegie Hall!

Paula's original version of her story was actually a journal entry, and her mother encouraged her to turn it into a short story. She found that, at times, writing in a journal was a negative experience for her, until she read an enlightening book. "I read Julia Cameron's The Artist's Way, *which helped me take a turn toward more positive journal writing and nurture my creative desires."*

The inspiration for this story is credited to her music teacher: "Shellie is a very talented woman who has a gift for sharing her love of music with students of all ages." Paula is now the proud owner of a new Yamaha conservatory grand piano. She says, "I will perform for anyone who will listen!"

It's Never Too Late, Is It?

Ann B. Sullivan

I sat there anxiously. It was my first time in a classroom since I had graduated from high school fourteen years earlier. In anticipation of getting lost my first time on campus, I had gotten off work an hour early. I was happy that I had only gotten slightly lost, but there I was, thirty-five minutes too early for class. I sat there, confidently at first. After all, I was an intelligent woman who would enjoy the adventure of returning to school. College would be fun, challenging even.

As the minutes passed and I was the only one sitting in the classroom, my mind started to run amok and my confidence waned. What had possessed me to think I was up to this challenge? What if I had taken on too much? What if I couldn't even pass my classes? What if school had changed too much since I had last attended and I couldn't fit in? What if it was too late in my life for this, if I had waited too long? What if . . .

Just as I was ready to bolt, terrified, out the door, never to return, a young man doing a strange chickenlike strut lurched in. The top of his pants was pulled up a little higher than his crotch, revealing blue boxer shorts. He was wearing an earring attached by a chain to his nose. Of course, with all the open seats to choose from, he threw himself into the one next to mine and grunted, "Am I supposed to be here?"

How was I to respond? Was this some psycho that was just looking for an excuse to take some weird repressed anger out on a cowering woman if she answered his question wrong? I had already been panicking from my own doing, so it was very hard to answer calmly.

"If you're supposed to be in Health Concepts, I believe you're in the right place."

"Cool!" was his almost innocent reply as he proceeded to lean back in his chair and nod off to sleep, a state in which he remained until the end of class.

As I was adjusting to this, a young lady strolled in, sporting a bright tattoo on her ankle and a diamond stud through the side of her nose. "Hey." She nodded in my direction as she chose a seat across the room. Again, not knowing how to respond, I just smiled nervously. I found myself wondering how foolish I would look if I started to cry.

Other students started filtering in. I tried, for the most part, to ignore them. "Hey," I heard exchanged many times. As I sat there, feeling completely deflated from having made the worst decision of my life, something dawned on me. "Hey" was simply a greeting that had replaced the traditional "Hi" that I was used to. For some reason, that realization brought me back to my senses. I had actually caught on to something that I hadn't known earlier. Granted, it was an extremely trivial bit of info — "Hey" instead of "Hi" — but it reminded me of the fact that I could change, too. That's what coming to college was all about in the first place, right? Enthusiastically, I waited to test my new theory, and, sure enough, the next person that strolled in the door looked in my direction.

"Hey." He nodded at me.

"Hey," I replied, sounding to myself as if I hadn't spoken in a million years. The young man hadn't picked up on the crackling in my voice, and he just smiled, contented that his greeting had been acknowledged, and walked past.

What a victory! Suddenly, I remembered all of the things I had told myself when I had decided to register for college. I remembered that I wasn't there to make new friends or to play dating games, I knew that I wouldn't be worried about peer pressure. Most of all, I remembered that I was there because I like to learn new things. I wasn't there to impress anyone — I was there for me. I was there to keep my brain from turning to Jell-O with the monotony of everyday life. I was there to make myself feel better about myself, and to learn a few new things in the process.

As the teacher walked into the room and the class turned its attention to forming first impressions about her, I happily concluded that I would be all right. I also knew that I would be back, next week as well as next semester. This was for me and I would enjoy every challenging minute of it. I was contented with the knowledge that to do something positive for myself, it is truly never too late.

Ann is happy to report that, after all her fear and uncertainty, she finished this class, as well as three others that semester, and had a 4.0 grade point average. She has been married for twelve years and values her husband's constant support as she travels through her phases of life. "I've always loved putting my thoughts on paper. I hope they will stir up ideas for someone who may be contemplating a big step and has doubts."

Taking Life
Less Seriously

Kelly Sollenberger

In the small space of twenty years, my outlook on life has evolved to one that most people probably never experience. I look around at the worried, uptight people in this world and want to shake some sense into them. There are endless choices and pleasures that nobody ever takes advantage of because people don't realize that life is only what one makes it. I live by several mottoes, the most important being that I can do whatever I want with my life, regardless of past patterns in society, and my choice is to have fun in everything that I do. I realize, of course, that this is much easier said than done; the biggest challenge in my life, therefore, is reminding myself to roll with the punches and take whatever opportunities life sends my way.

Three years ago, I had my first grown-up thought: I am not happy with my life right now, so why the hell don't I change it? The best thing I've done for myself so far is finding a way to make myself happy in all aspects of life. I moved to a city I love, I became friends with people whom I love, and each day I wake up and go to a school that I love. After that, I go to a job that I love, hang out with the friends whom I love, and if it turns out to be a lousy day anyway, I sit back and try to forget about it. There's no fun in stressing over a bad day (well, at least for more than half an hour over coffee with your best friend), and, more importantly, it doesn't help. I may be young, but I'm not naïve — my life has been a bowl of cherries, and I have yet to experience the tragedy of death, but I want to be able to look back on my short life and say that I lived it to the fullest no matter what was thrown my way. Keeping an open mind and trying whatever I think will broaden my horizons are surefire techniques to reach this goal. It's important to remember not to get bogged down by daily hassles. Don't sweat the small stuff.

Life moves very fast. If you don't stop to enjoy it, you could miss it entirely. Becoming the unique person you want to be and trying every single stupid thing you've ever wanted to try are the best way to grab life by the horns and enjoy yourself. I refuse to die without ever having shouted my joy from the top of the Eiffel Tower or without baring my soul with reckless abandon to someone I love but who may not love me back. I will not lie on my deathbed and say that I was stuck in a job I hated for ten years because it paid well, or that I never made that random trip to Brazil because work and family obligations got in the way. I will make time for whatever will fulfill my dreams, and I will know that having a full life doesn't allow me to worry about the annoying hurdles of everyday life. An upbeat outlook and the capacity for self-forgiveness will keep my life moving along quite nicely.

Life is just a series of interruptions. We might as well accept these interruptions and look at them as points from which to improve our current situation. So what if the man of your dreams cheats on you a week before the wedding? His older brother is much cuter anyway (you know, the one who is attracted to you and your zest for life)! Dwelling on this jerk for too long will only make you miss out on something better. Remember that.

I'm just glad that I have stumbled upon this knowledge this early in my life. For those of you who are just now realizing that the secret to life is simply to do whatever you want with it, don't fret over lost years. Just pick up your life now and do all that you can with whatever time you have left. Take that gondola ride underneath the Bridge of Sighs with your sweetheart, and don't think twice about missing a week or two of work. Isn't it more important to accomplish a dream? Carpe diem! And never go to bed unless you have a great story to tell the next morning. What fun would life be without that?

Currently a college student, Kelly was prompted to write this piece after seeing so many "unhappy people, of all ages, who weren't enjoying their lives." Kelly believes the key to fulfilling your dreams is your outlook, and she credits her family for nurturing her beliefs. Her motto for life comes from the Indigo Girls: "The best thing you've ever done for me is to help me take my life less seriously; it's only life, after all."

Remembering
with
Love

A Birthday Wish

Melissa Webb

Our eyes met as I blew out my candles. I made my wish, Dad. I wished for a how-to book — a wonderful book full of simple instructions, and helpful hints, about how to survive life after Dad.

Chapter 1 should explain how a story carries on without its main character: how birthdays can still be celebrated, turkeys carved, and joy found in Christmas carols.

Chapter 2 might list strategies for finding a new best friend. Someone with your wisdom who knows when to give advice and when to listen.

Chapter 3 would probably list ingredients on your recipe for courage. Step-by-step instructions would show me how you managed everything from my reckless independence to dealing with your body's battle with cancer.

Chapter 4 could include lessons on simply being grateful for treasured memories: to once again walk along the beach, share a sunset, or talk quietly over lunch.

And finally, Chapter 5 would show me reasons to smile again. It would teach me that I only need to look inside myself to find you. It would leave me with the knowledge that my life has been blessed for having known you, the man who is my dad.

"I wrote this story to honor the wonderful relationship my dad and I have shared over the years; because of his health problems in recent years, I cherish our time together." To live so many years knowing he was always there for her is something Melissa does not take for granted. Her husband and son are great fans of her stories. "My husband and son patiently read and comment (favorably, of course) on my writing." She finds inspiration in traveling and likes nothing better than a good thunderstorm and a mystery book.

Fragrance of Love

Vickie Elaine Legg

I pulled her worn purse from the closet and un-zipped it, savoring the familiar fragrances as hot tears stung my eyes. For as long as I can re-member, my mother's purses have smelled of White Shoulders perfume and spearmint chew-ing gum.

Over the years, there were dozens, all shapes and colors of the rainbow, but none rivaled the memory of this black leather shoulder bag. She carried it the year she retired.

We argued about everything in those days.

"Why don't you wait to buy groceries until I come with the car?" I asked.

"I manage just fine," she said, gesturing to a two-wheeled shopping cart she pulled behind her when she walked the four blocks to the gro-cery store. "Besides, you're bossy. You tell me how to shop."

"Oh, Mother. Just because I tried to save you money on trash bags, you think I'm telling you how to shop?"

"You were. I don't like cheap trash bags. I like thick ones."

"I know. You like super-duper, heavy-duty green ones with red drawstring ties."

We both laughed.

One Wednesday, in April, Mom walked to the store. To keep the sacks from tearing on the metal cart, she placed one of the thick green trash bags inside.

After unloading the groceries, she heard a knock at the door. Ever cautious, she looked for a hiding place for her purse, dropped it into the cart, and forgot about it.

The next day, my brother Tim stopped by. Before leaving, he asked, "Mom, want me to take your trash to the collection bin?"

"Oh, would you? I have one bag ready, but I need to empty the wastebasket."

"Don't bother getting up. I can do it," Tim said, heading for the kitchen. "Looks like you're out of bags." Then he added, "No problem. I'll use the one in the cart."

Friday morning, Mom missed her purse. She looked everyplace she usually hid it — under the mattress, in the washer, in the clothes hamper.

I was summoned by her frantic telephone call. "It's gone. My whole life was in there!"

We searched for hours.

"Try to think where you had it last," I said, lifting the dust ruffle on her bed.

"I never put it under there. That's the first place a thief would look," she said, hands on her hips.

I sighed. "If we don't find it, it's not the end of the world."

She shook her head. "My whole life is in there

— my checkbook, four hundred dollars, my emerald ring."

"Why would you carry that much cash and the ring in the purse?"

Her blue eyes flashed. "I had just been to the bank. I like to keep a little cash on hand. I took the ring off in church Sunday when my fingers swelled. I guess I forgot to put it away."

"Seems like you're forgetting a lot of things lately."

She glared.

Early the next morning, she called, her voice singing, "I remember where I put it!"

"That's great. Where?"

"I dropped it in the grocery cart. Tim must have used the trash bag and thrown it away. Come quickly."

The burly man at the collection site pointed with a grubby hand toward a huge, smelly trash-compactor truck. "If it come in yesterday, it's in there and it ain't goin' nowhere 'til Monday. That's when I drive the baby to the county dump. You can go over there on Monday and look, if you like."

Mom beamed. "We'll be there."

I shook my head. "Why don't you just call it a loss? We'll never find it in all that trash."

She squared her shoulders. "If that's the way you feel, young lady, your sister will take me."

Monday morning brought April showers. Mom and my sister, Nancy, clad in raincoats, boots, and yellow rubber gloves waited like vultures at the county landfill for the trash truck to dump its load. It crept along, spreading a reeking carpet of smashed trash bags over the muddy ground.

Nancy sighed, "How will we ever find it?"

Mom smiled. "I use good bags. Look for the heavy-duty green ones with red drawstrings."

Nancy began dragging the possibilities to the edge while Mom opened them and picked through the contents with a stick.

When she opened the sixth bag, she cried, "This one's mine!" There at the bottom was her purse, smashed but otherwise intact.

Later, she told me with a smile, "If I had listened to you, I never would have found it. I had to keep looking — my whole life was in there."

My heart ached as I caressed the worn leather. Then I slid the zipper shut, hoarding the sweet, comforting fragrances as if *my* whole life was in there.

After a brief terrifying illness, Vickie's mother passed away. Writing this story afforded her additional means of mourning her mother's death and, through her humor and poignancy, honoring her mother. Vickie is the mother of three and stepmother of three, though all but one are grown. She is a former teacher, and now she has time to travel with her husband, Floyd.

Orange Blossoms in the Misty Morning

Nancy Robards Thompson

My mother died in the spring and left me in a cold void. The days were so warm, so beautiful. The blue sky and golden sun seemed mocking and cruel, a joke understood by everyone but me. Only after deep reflection did I realize it was the universe's way of celebrating her life and the deep love we shared.

Memories grow dim as I try to recall her face. I strain to remember her smile before she grew so tired, before we fought, because I thought she was giving up. She was always the brave one, everyone's source of strength. How I wish I had been stronger for her in those days.

We would debate life over steaming cups of tea. She implored me to not prolong the inevitable when the time came that she could no longer sustain. I would indignantly try to turn her to my way of thinking. "I will always do everything possible to keep you alive," I said. Puffed up in my self-righteousness, I never truly believed she would go. She had always been there. She wouldn't do that to *me*.

It was always about me, until reality hit. I

couldn't bear to watch her suffer, and through streaming tears, I bid her a peaceful farewell. Now I bask in the memories of the love and good times we shared and try to forgive myself for being a child not wanting to let go. We loved more than most people do in a lifetime, and I take time to pause each day to remember the things that mattered to her and the uniqueness that made her special — the crisp smell of her perfume; the sound of waves gently breaking on the shore, how the ebb and flow of the tide would put her at ease, gently melting away tension; the scent of orange blossoms in the misty morning as we drove along open stretches of highway with windows down, just to breathe in the heady scent. We didn't have to talk. Carefree in her calm, I would prop my elbow on the door and arm-wrestle the rushing air. . . . I feel her presence when a gentle breeze caresses my cheek. . . . She catches me by surprise when I catch glimpses of her in my reflection, or hear her voice in my own. . . . She's with me always.

She instilled in me a sense of worth and spirit — an inner strength that is every woman's birthright. She gave me wings yet had the courage to let go when I wanted to fly. And I am eternally grateful for this unconditional love. This love shaped my life and gave me the strength to live side by side in equality with my partner.

For years, I pondered how I might repay the debt for the bounty of love she so freely bestowed upon me. For years, I was at a loss, until my husband and I brought a daughter of our own into the world. Now it's clear I must carry on this legacy of love, patience, and understanding. Teach my daughter to live with no regrets and drink in the scent of the orange blossoms as soon as they bloom. They wither and fade all too fast, especially in the spring. . . .

Nancy wrote this story as a tribute to her mother, who died ten years ago. "The idea came to me when, early this spring, our daughter asked where the pretty white flowers on the orange tree had gone. It dawned on me how strange it was that while all the other flowers were thriving, the orange blossoms were fading." Nancy's mother always loved the way the blossoms would perfume the air and, to this day, Nancy can't smell that scent without thinking of her mother.

My Mother — Myself

Kristina Cliff-Evans

Today is October twenty-fifth, and I am fifty-one years old. No, it isn't my birthday; that happened back in February. What it is is the twenty-fourth anniversary of my mother's death. She was fifty-one when she died. I remember it all too clearly, that last day of her life — a rainy Monday in the hospital — how she couldn't breathe.

"It's fluid," the resident said. "We'll tap her lungs." And they did. They sat her up in the hospital bed, draped her, and plunged the long needle through her back into her lungs — again and again — but no fluid came, no relief.

"It's *not* fluid," the resident said. "It's all tumor. We can't help her breathe."

I remember her words: "I can't . . . breathe. Turn up the oxygen . . . please," over and over. We did. It didn't help. Her lungs, bursting with cancer, fought, struggled to make room for the life-sustaining oxygen. They couldn't do it — there was *no room left.*

I remember my mother's final words to me, whispered: "I want the quickest way."

But I have digressed. . . . I am fifty-one. She was fifty-one. My mother should have grown old. Her dark hair, peppered with gray, should have gradually become snowy white. The fine lines etched in her face from her smiles should have become soft wrinkles. Her quick step should have given way over the years to a slower, more elderly gait. Her constant effervescent activity — mostly volunteer — should have mellowed into the gentle pace of the "sweet old lady who's always there helping out."

She should have watched her five grandchildren grow up; should have had the chance to enfold them in her very special brand of love; been able to impart to them her considerable wisdom. She should have been arm in arm with my father, as the only girl he ever loved, traveling into a shared old age.

She didn't; she wasn't. She never had the chance. She was fifty-one and she died. I was twenty-seven when my mother died. Over the years, not a day has gone by in which I don't think of something I want to tell my mother, to ask her, or to show her. Mostly, that thought is followed by another: Oh, I can't — of course. Sometimes, though, when the need is great — great hurt, great worry, great pain, great joy — I rail bitterly against the utter injustice of it all. It wasn't *and isn't* right that I could not, did not, *and do not* have my mother!

Now I am fifty-one. I look into the mirror, or at a picture of myself, and it strikes me: I have slowly but surely been transformed. There *she* is with that gray-peppered hair, those intense dark eyes, that expression I also have; or when I hear my own voice — her voice — I have become my mother. She stands beside me — my own age. She never grew any older than I am now. I am dumbfounded.

In a few months, I will enter a completely new and strange stage of my life. I will begin to be older than my mother. From that point on, the direction in which I gaze to see her will change. I have always looked ahead to see her. Amazingly, now I stand next to her — now briefly I am merged with her. Soon I will look back at my mother. Slowly, she will become young in comparison to me. I will grow old, instead of her — acquire the white hair she should have had (but never did). I will develop the elderly gait she never experienced, see those soft wrinkles (she never had) in my face. And so it will continue — on and on, until one day when I am seventy-five, as she would have been today. On that day, the extraordinary reversal of our roles complete, I will turn around to look at her, but see, instead, my own daughter, at fifty-one — my mother.

Kristina was prompted to write this story just before her fifty-second birthday — the birthday her mother never had. "This would be the start of a whole new chapter, and I did not want it to pass unnoticed." She wanted to explore feelings, and attitudes toward living beyond her mother's life span.

Kristina lives with her husband, Kenneth, and

is the mother of three children. She is in the early stages of career number three, as a freelance writer and consultant.

The Faint Fluttering of Wings

Zelpha Denise Smith

Diann and I go to see our parents together these days. When we present a united front, we are particularly invincible. Since we found out Dad has lung cancer and is dying, my sister and I have gained at least fifteen pounds a piece. Put that much extra poundage into play and your foes might as well be facing two Mack trucks with headlights and engines gunning to go.

Mom is still smoking outside, away from Dad's labored breathing, which does a lot for Diann's blood pressure and keeps me in God's good graces. There are only so many times you can think about dropping your mother with a single shot before lightning strikes you straight down.

Dad is in pain. His motions are exaggerated as he moves slowly. When Diann and I first walk in and watch him shuffle out of his favorite chair, I see the same fear I feel reflected in my sister's eyes. When I put my arms around him and offer my familiar and falsely bright "Hi, Pop," I feel as though I am holding something fragile — like a bird with a broken wing. Dad must feel it, too, because at the slightest touch, he cringes like a frightened animal intent on avoiding further harm. I kiss his head, and his scalp smells like the skin of so many of the patients I use to accompany in the ambulance. It is the smell of a long, tiring illness. Maybe it is also a whiff of death passing through the house, settling on my father's head — I don't know, but sometimes I want him to be better so much that it hurts my heart. These are the moments when I close my eyes and feel the dark emptiness of my father's loss washing over me like the giant waves we used to brave along the California coastline.

Diann is glib and giggly. She teases my father with the ease of someone who knows him well. She has always been his confidante, but we are both my father's daughters. He loves us with intensity, sometimes fueled by guilt, but mostly stoked by his determination to never let us down again. He feels as though he often has, and there are no words left to say to make him see that we love him for who he is.

Diann and I map out our strategies before we even pull into our parents' drive. "You say this," and "I'll say that," my sister and I tell each other. We orchestrate conversations with my parents like dancers verbally spinning and dipping until we've covered all the important topics without ever uttering a serious word. Diann uses the joking approach best. Her eyes glitter as she says to Dad, "You know you have to eat, or you'll walk right out of your pants." I follow her lead as easily as twirling to an inaudible beat. "You know, Dad," I say, "hope when they take that stitch out of your back, your arm doesn't fall off." Our parents appreciate this approach. We came from a long line of people in denial, and we are intent on upholding the family tradition — at least with them.

In the car on the way home, Diann shares a new CD with me. Soon we are both crying. We have seen the first traces of death casting shadows around my father's eyes and now we know the end will come. We aren't good at sharing our tears, so we try to keep them inside, but they spill out onto our cheeks. Sobs rise from our chests like hiccups, and when we realize that we are sobbing in stereo, we both begin to laugh and cry at the same time.

One song ends and another begins as we round the bend through town. This song is about shedding your tears, which sends us right into another bout of hilarious despair. The icing on the cake is the hearse sitting under the red light. We have come directly upon the beginning of a funeral procession. The irony is too obvious to miss. A long line of cars with their lights on makes a slow trek through the intersection and we try to catch our breath but only manage to smile, frown, laugh, cry.

"Boy, our guardian angels sure do have some sense of humor," we gasp. It's true. Throughout this entire ordeal, we've often heard the faint fluttering of wings and felt the comforting presence of those God has entrusted to watch over sisters and other hard-and-fast friends. That is what will see us through — our angels and each other.

The day after her father's memorial service, Zelpha received my notice that her story had been accepted. She said, "I know my father would be proud of me — he always encouraged me to be whatever I wanted to be." Her story was written for all women who have found the courage to walk to the end of life with a loved one. "I know it was the hardest thing I've ever done. Thank God for my sister and the ever-present faint fluttering of 'angel wings.'" She and her sister had been close prior to their father's illness; however, their bond grew deeper through their sadness. Together, they braced their father's attitude, made peace with him, and said good-bye as he died at his home.

Independent
Woman

Fighting Discrimination with Dignity

Paula E. Buford, Th.P.

I learned how to fight discrimination with dignity the day that I broke into the all-male Southern Baptist pastors' conference in 1984. It was not without trepidation that I accepted an invitation to speak on being a "Woman in Ministry." I would be the first ordained Baptist woman that most of these Jacksonville, Florida, ministers had ever met. Consequently, I expected to bear the brunt of their unconscious conflicts with women in authority. And theologically, I shattered the notion that men held the exclusive right to represent a "male" God.

I was new at representing myself in public, having been ordained for only about a year and having only two years of experience as a hospital chaplain. What is a Baptist female minister supposed to be like? I was constantly asking myself as I invented my life day by day.

The atmosphere was tense among Southern Baptists nationwide as more and more women like myself were becoming ordained and were seeking out roles previously available only to men. I expected a hostile audience, so I began to talk about my commonality with these men. "Like many of you, I grew up in the church and I remember hearing, over and over, from the Baptist teachings that I was created in the image of God; that the spirit of God would help me interpret the Scriptures for myself; that I should follow God's leading, even when it was unpopular and misunderstood; that I should use my spiritual gifts in ministry to help others. My gifts are in the area of support and encouragement, and chaplaincy is a natural ministry for me, one that requires ordination."

That said, I talked about some of my poignant hospital experiences, in which my presence as a woman seemed significant. Then very reluctantly, I asked, "Does anyone have any questions?" As I waited for a moment, I imagined a lynch mob rising up to punish me for my hysterical beliefs. And I was not entirely wrong in my expectation.

"As a woman, how will you keep from being seen as a sex object in the pulpit?" an elderly pastor asked with hostility.

I worked hard to maintain composure. You see, Baptist pastors are notoriously admired by the ladies, and they often promote physical intimacy by hugging and flirting with their female church members. Many of them are charismatic pulpiteers; others act as the most nurturing male in a lonely woman's life.

I paused and thanked God for my non-threatening presence. At age thirty-two, I looked all of twenty and weighed one hundred pounds soaking wet. In an evenhanded tone, I responded, "I'm not sure that I can. Tell me, how do you deal with this issue? I'd like to learn from you."

At that, he huffed, sputtered, and sat down. After all, it was only these wanton would-be women preachers who lured their flock down the path of sin.

Another question boomed out. "I recently intervened in a life-and-death situation late at night. Jack, a church member, was holding a loaded gun to his wife's head, and I had to talk him out of shooting his wife and maybe himself. How could a defenseless woman like you handle a situation like that?"

I again paused at the absurdity of the question. Why would any fool want to go rushing into a situation like that? He sounded like a medieval knight charging to the defense of a damsel in distress. But again, I took a deep breath and waited until I was calm and levelheaded before responding. In my silence, a brother leapt up.

"Why, I wouldn't handle a situation like that myself, and I am a man!"

There was a great rumbling among the brethren. Some were shaking their heads with shame at the sexist question; others were angry and bewildered over what to do with me and the bedlam that was mounting. If this had been the Wild West, a barroom brawl would have commenced.

No longer the "exhibit" for the day, I sat down

before any more verbal missiles could be launched at me, and I chuckled at my good fortune. I actually survived this speech without throttling anyone. I guess I can survive just about anywhere!

That day, I learned that injustice and prejudice are best met by simple dignity and understanding. I continued to attend those ministerial meetings as a regular member, and by the end of the year, I became a person, instead of an adversary, to many of those men.

Paula sustained a traumatic brain injury in a 1992 auto accident, and she has shifted the focus of her ministry. She now has a ministry called Earthen Vessels, which involves academic research and creating handmade pottery with spiritual imagery. Paula expressed her future plans this way: "I hope to offer integrative workshops that combine pottery, therapy, and spirituality for persons with disabilities, and for ministers who need to learn how to play."

Looking Back...But Moving On

Oona'o Haynes

It felt eerie driving past my house. *My house*, it wasn't my house anymore. It was an empty house on a block where I used to live. I couldn't help glancing in the rearview mirror for one more peek. The yard was in disarray — the grass overgrown, the bushes dry and haggard-looking. I sighed. It used to be so beautiful. Neglect had taken over in just a few short months. No use looking back. That was then, and this is now, I told myself.

I reminded myself where I was going. To a job, in a car. When I first got the job at the extended-care facility, I didn't have a car. I barely had bus fare. Generally, things were a little better. I smiled to myself. Now I had a new job and a used car. Sure, it paid less per hour than what I was accustomed to earning. I was out of my field and I had to punch a time clock — something I had never experienced before. I had always been the boss, even before I started my own business. I resolved to deal with the present. I was no longer a home owner, no longer the president/CEO of my own typesetting/graphic arts company. Without warning, severe circumstances had changed everything in the blink of an eye. It was time to move forward. I didn't have the luxury of looking back.

I pulled into the parking lot and turned the engine off. For a few minutes, I sat looking at the huge building that housed a segment of the population that was often forgotten by family, friends, and society itself.

Getting off the elevator on my unit, the smell of cleaning agents and medications hit my nostrils. I heard Barbara, one of the patients, screaming down the hall. Periodically, she would scream for several minutes and then abruptly stop. "Good morning, Mrs. Coombs. How are you?" I asked. She looked up at me. "There, there — they are trying to do it again," she yelled. "Get them out of here! They're always trying to come in here to get in my bed! Oh, God, please, somebody, make them leave me alone!" I looked around the room. Although I saw no one, or anything, I agreed with her. "You're right. Something has to be done about this!" I exclaimed. I sat down on the bed next to her and began to yell at imaginary intruders. "You get out of here right now! I do not, under any circumstances, want to see you in this room again. Furthermore, if you dare come back, I will have you arrested!" Mrs Coombs looked at me; I looked at her. She started laughing. "Boy, you sure told them! I bet they won't be back," she said. Gently, I got off the bed, inviting her to the morning greeting and exercise circle. Heading toward the door, I said, "You know, we really do enjoy having you exercise with us." She smiled and said, "I wouldn't miss it for the world."

Walking down the west wing, I noticed Mr. Polo's shirt was caught in the spoke of his wheelchair. He was struggling to get it loose. "Here, let me help you." I pulled the material gently away from the wheel. "I bet one of the women did that on purpose just to slow you down. Trying to catch a good man is hard," I joked. He frowned and replied angrily, "Shucks, girl, don't nobody want no one-legged man." Despite his gruff response, I could tell he was pleased. He seemed to sit up straighter; like he still had something to offer life.

Finished with my morning room visits, I proceeded toward the solarium to set up my schedule for the day. Little by little, patients, young and old alike, were beginning to filter into the large room. Each one had a special need and a story to tell. It was my job as a therapeutic recreation therapist to meet those needs — to give them a reason to get up in the morning.

Opening the door to my apartment after a long day, I thanked God for my health, my mind, and the opportunity to be in charge of my life. I didn't have to wait for someone to take me to the bathroom or give me pain medication just to make it through the day. I didn't have to wonder if anybody loved me. I had family and friends. I had the privilege of starting each new day with potential and choices.

Oona'o was inspired to write this story when she lost her business, could not find new employment, and her husband was unjustly incarcerated. She believes that sometimes closed doors are opportunities to change your adventure in life.

She has gone on to become a certified aromatherapist and herbalist and is pursuing her doctorate in naturopathy. The mother of two "beautiful daughters," she concludes, "We all have a story to tell. We just need someone to listen."

Launched

Mary Anne Butler

It only took a week, but I grew in those seven days from a nurtured child to a woman. I was eighteen. It was time, although I was unprepared for the bats that were swung at me by strangers my mother had warned me about as she put me on the train bound for Baltimore that July morning in 1943.

By week's end, my landlady had thrown me out of the house for wearing shorts and for sneaking an extra bath. "Only three a week allowed," she said in that authoritative manner old people use with the young. "Indecent," she said of the shorts.

I quickly found another room in a poorer part of town, where row houses prevailed. But more trouble lay ahead.

My father had arranged my employment as a file clerk at the Maryland Drydock Company, a Baltimore shipyard. He was friendly with a man who knew a relative of the purchasing agent. No one inquired about my skills. Bound for college until my Depression-plagued family decided there was no money, I now found that my one semester of high school typing did not prepare me for success at this wartime working girl job. I never learned to type the numbers on the type-writer and so many of them were used to make up the fraction-studded specifications for the davits and widgets, pipes and fittings used to make disabled ships seaworthy again. My hesitant fingers creeping over those numeric keys left sticky patches of dampness; my eyes burned like hot coals; my neck developed a crick.

"You're wasting too much paper," my boss, Mr. Forrest, yelled from his desk, where he sat like a stern schoolmaster. "Don't you know a misplaced number could sink a ship?" And every one of those thirty employees, sitting like school-children at their grown-up desks, heard. "Report to the files immediately," he bellowed.

Failure clamped me in its steely claws, for no position in office hierarchy rates lower than a file clerk. My throat muscles bunched. I fought the tears, but that night alone on my bed, I let them loose like rain in a monsoon until a saving thought occurred. Those files were a mess. Purchase orders for tankers nested in files for troop ships; paperwork for ships long gone to the ocean floor languished in the active files. I could clean them up. The next morning, I started with the *A*'s.

A few weeks later, Mr. Forrest stopped by my windowless file room to say, "You're doing a great job. How would you like to be an invoice checker?" Would I? The gods had truly blessed me. Only men were invoice checkers.

He assigned me to Mr. Curtis, a blue-eyed,

dark-haired romeo who had already caught me among the files and given me a few squeezes. Once, he even kissed me full on the lips. That he was married seemed no deterrent. Mr. Curtis explained that before payments to suppliers could be made, every item received had to be checked against its companion on the purchase order. I now had my own file and a desk in front of a window — two sure signs of achievement. This gave me full view of the yard, where torn-up ships were being refitted and repaired. One, the *Leonardo da Vinci*, a confiscated Italian luxury liner, had been brought in with her buxom lady figurehead still searching the seas, carved hair flowing in make-believe wind. Workers cut her down first, for the *da Vinci* was destined to become a gleaming white hospital ship, soon to be renamed *Refuge*. Her ornate appointments and gilded mirrors were carried from elegant salons, to be replaced by operating rooms and sick bays.

For the six months that I watched her progress, I also watched my pay envelope for signs of a raise, and once boldly asked Mr. Curtis if he was making much more than my weekly twenty-two-dollar file clerk's salary. "More than twice." He laughed. "But girls can't expect to be paid as much as men."

I was bolder now, and every payday I planted myself firmly before Mr. Forrest's desk and asked, "Where is it?"

"It's coming," he'd promise, adding, "We're very pleased with your work."

"I can't live on pleasure," I said, stalking off.

The next payday, two dollars more per week appeared in my pay envelope. So when the great white ship with her green stripe and red cross slipped out of dry dock to begin her search for wounded and dying boys in bloodied Atlantic waters, I decided it was time to go, too. Knowing that I could hold a job, I borrowed six hundred dollars from an aunt and enrolled in college. Not only would I pay her back but I would gain skills that would take me away from filing and invoice checking, and maybe someday an employer would pay me like a man.

Mary Anne graduated from college with a degree in arts and letters, and a major in journalism. "Although I am now retired, I was, until two years ago, a public relations consultant for a national trade association. And for thirteen years, I was copy director for a national fund-raising and public relations firm."

Mary Anne has been married for forty-six years and she and her husband have three grown children and two grandchildren.

The Businesswoman

Pamela Martin

This past May, I celebrated my twentieth year in the printing business. Well, I didn't actually celebrate; I was just keenly aware of this milestone anniversary. And the prevailing thought throughout the day was, twenty years is long enough to do anything. However, here I am, almost a year later, still in the printing business.

It all began when my former employer asked me to become his partner in a new venture. He had sold his original business, had divorced, and was ready to start his life over. I was twenty-two, in college (for the first time in my life), and thrilled that he thought enough of me to ask me to join him in the business. He, of course, was the decision maker; I was his support system.

Cliff and I worked eighty-hour weeks during our first year, for minimal pay, then decided that we should probably pool our resources and simplify our lives. We were spending nearly every minute of every day together, so the logical thing was to get married. We did!

The next four years were full of hard work and success. They also brought the birth of our daughter and the purchase of our first home. We were richly rewarded for our efforts and life was wonderful. Then in May of 1981, my husband (and business partner) was diagnosed with testicular cancer. I will never forget sinking to the floor when the doctor pronounced that diagnosis. Our wonderful life was coming to a crashing halt!

That was the moment my life started changing. I was immediately forced into caring for our children (our daughter and his son by a previous marriage), tending to our home, and running our business *by myself,* all in the midst of trying to care for the man I loved, who was critically ill. I went from *being* the support system to *needing* one . . . and having to develop one! For three years, my husband underwent surgery, radiation, and radical chemotherapy treatments. While his world consisted of trying to survive physically, mine consisted of trying to survive in every other way.

I had never planned to own my own business, and even when I joined him as a partner, I didn't really think of the business as mine. It was his; I was just there to help. But through those years of hardship, I learned and I survived. When Cliff began to get well (a miracle, by all accounts), he didn't see a need to return to our business. I was doing just fine without him, so he decided to do something entirely different. He bought a marina (his lifelong dream).

Three years later, Cliff and I separated. Our lives, which once had been so intertwined, had grown completely apart and it was difficult for him to accept his "new" wife: a woman of action, with opinions. Three years later, we divorced, resigned to the fact that we could not "go back" and that our lives had been forever changed.

But the one constant in my life has been my business. Since I had never planned to run my own company, I had not studied business in college; in fact, I didn't even finish college. I had not taken courses or seminars on how to manage; I just learned as I went along. What I did do was base my business philosophy on my life philosophy — to treat people as I wished to be treated. In that vein, I have developed hundreds of relationships in which I always keep in mind the best interests of my customers. Often, in the process, I have cost myself business or additional profit, but my customers have grown to trust me. Sixty-five percent of my customers today are the same ones I began with twenty-one years ago. Several of them have grown into large businesses; some have remained small and independent; many have sent new customers to me, and often, when my business world is suffering, it is those people who rally and come to *my* support (some even dream up work to send me when times are bad).

So while I do not necessarily fit the image of today's businesswoman, I am a woman in business today — all because of the hand life dealt me. Not by choice or design did I end up where I am, but out of necessity. And now, when my industry is dying a slow death and I find myself questioning my future, I know that somehow I will find the way to survive.

Pamela says, "The writing of the story brought back painful memories of a difficult time, but it also made me realize that that time was, in a large part, what shaped the past twenty years of my life. It also made me realize that I am in fact a sur- vivor — someone who can take the hand life deals them and make the best of it."

Pamela feels grateful for all the "hard times" and is still in the printing business. Her nineteen- year-old daughter recently told her, "Mom, I'm becoming you!" When Pamela asked if that was a bad thing, her daughter said she would be proud to be like her. "That comment alone was enough to make me feel that my entire life has been a great success!"

The Woman on Flight Number 862

V. B. Rhode

Speed of flight number 862: Mach 0.80
Passenger's heart rate: 160 beats per minute

She stepped aboard flight number 862 at nine o'clock on a Monday morning, a victim of spousal abuse. As the flight swooped low over the Washington Monument, she bookmarked the moment. What is a nice girl like me doing in an airplane landing at National Airport, Washington, D.C.?

I was that woman. Several weeks earlier, I had received a wake-up call. In an incident of domestic violence very similar to my own, a local woman was found dead.

After eight years of coping with his jealousy and drunken fury, which always left me bruised, I knew what I had to do: leave.

I learned the hard way not to believe the promises of an abuser. Four times, I had left my husband. He would get very depressed and say it wouldn't happen again. Then I felt sorry for him and went back home.

No, the only way to divorce this man (and live

through it) was to move out — out of the state. To do that, I had to get a job with a company that had offices outside California.

A company selling Yellow Pages advertising that had offices in California, Kansas City, and Virginia offered me a job, with the possibility of transfer to another state. Things didn't work out just as I'd hoped — but much better. While in Kansas City for three weeks of intensive training, I learned that angels really do exist. Cleverly disguised as my roommate, an angel named Mickey virtually saved my life.

"Well, Mickey, I have an ulterior motive in taking this job. You see, I have to get out of California — because of my husband." The next day, the personnel director called me into his office to discuss my "personal problem" — Thanks loads, Mickey! I suppose they'll fire me now — and since he needed a new salesperson on the East Coast, would I like to go to Virginia?

What? Go where? Virginia? Now? I accepted.

As flight number 862 approached National Airport, the landing gear clunked out of the jet's underbelly. The noise reminded me of my landing gear — or lack thereof. My entire support system — family and friends — was in California. I didn't know anyone east of San Bernardino! My temples throbbed.

Pressure of jet cabin: 8 pounds psi
My emotions: 1 million psi

I was about to escape the rites of domestic violence. Am I ready? Can I do this?

My journey back to a normal life would soon begin. Attractive and intelligent, I didn't fit the profile of a "typical" battered wife — or so I thought. Later, I discovered that both my husband and I exemplified such personality types. But, as I stepped off flight number 862, I still thought of myself as a lonely little petunia in the onion patch of domestic violence!

How did I make the transition from Battered Betty to Never Again Nellie? The first step was by learning to be responsible for only three individuals: me, myself and I. Pampering myself with bubble baths, romance novels, and Popsicles (okay, okay, chocolate chip ice cream at first), I found my own way of being strong. Gradually, I understood that I could never be responsible for his uncontrolled anger. Finally, I could be objective. I began thinking rationally and effectively about the future. I charted a course for tomorrow — all my tomorrows — without worry about offending or pleasing anyone else.

Flight plan: To work toward goals of my choice by using good judgment to make the best-possible choices

Networking with other single people who knew what they wanted helped me begin working toward my goals. Upbeat people and cheerful activities were supplied by a local church. A women's support group shared ways of making better choices by learning to identify alternatives.

The library became my home away from home. Its peaceful atmosphere offered a safe haven — at the right price! I read everything on the shelves about domestic violence; my experience was not unique:

Fifty percent of all women have been or will be assaulted by a spouse or boyfriend at least once during their life.

About 1.8 million American women are beaten by the men they live with.

Only one out of ten instances of wife abuse is reported.

Of every five hundred divorces, 57.4% involve battered wives.

Batterers include physicians, police officers, public officials, attorneys, et cetera.

Although such information didn't change my past, it was comforting to know that I was not alone.

Selling Yellow Page advertisements became my main focus. I didn't look for dates — that would take a while. By the time I did, I knew the danger signs.

Like my husband, batterers usually appear successful and fun-loving to outsiders. Men who want a lot of power, such as fast cars, beautiful women, and winning teams, have the potential for violence. Men who seem passive can change under stress, becoming combative adversaries. That I didn't need. That I'd had plenty of.

I'm not the same woman who stepped off flight number 862 that spring morning so long ago, but I remember her well. A sister in spirit, I am no longer a victim, but a victor in life.

Ms. Rhode is now happily remarried. In retrospect, she remains mystified as to why she put up with abuse for so long. This is her first story about her years as a battered woman. "I hope that my experience will convince other women that staying in an abusive relationship is a form of codependency, enabling their abuser to continue a sick behavior. Guilt, fear, and anxiety will give way to hope, confidence, and happiness within minutes of making a break."

The Power of Departure

Isabelle Hart

Mesmerized by the return of your exuberance for life, you faintly hear the chimes at Roissy Airport dissolving like droplets of rain in an ocean of voyagers. The muffled noise of hundreds of travelers walking, talking, ruffling papers, shutting their cases, and zipping their bags takes you further from your life. The speaker announces an imminent departure for Bangkok, Havana, or Tokyo, a departure that has nothing to do with you or your destination but which gives you that incredible feeling you have some power over your life and the world. Departure: a world at hand, filled with promises of new horizons, of a different world moving at a different pace.

The thought of returning to self with an inner peace found on this voyage, renewed and redirected, is equally empowering. It is the excitement of knowing that for a while you will register in your mind a thousand images, sounds, and colors that do not match your palette. Vulnerable yet wide awake, you are making yourself ready to swallow up everything your mind and body can take as far as sensations are concerned. It is the promise of an unknown, the thrill of waking up on foreign ground, the joy of discovery, and the power you have found within to just leave. It is the knowledge that if you decide you want to, you can be walking in a jungle, crossing a desert or wandering down a busy street at night. Maybe you're leaving for a new life, a new love, a new situation, where departure is required in order to return home to your happiness. None of it would be possible without the departure, this magic moment where you leave everything behind, where suddenly the most important thing in the world is finding the gate, making sure your ticket is in your pocket along with your passport. It is the foolish feeling that you have forgotten something and that none of the people you've left behind will be able to survive without you. And in the back of your mind, the certainty that nothing has been forgotten and that everyone will be all right. You stick to material things because you cannot picture what is waiting for you at the end of this passage in your life. You check your time of departure twenty times and keep looking for the ticket, which for some mysterious reason keeps changing location: from your pocket to your purse and back in your pocket. This passport of acceptance and validation of who you are and this ticket are your most precious belongings; they are your future and key to departure. To kill time, which has a tendency to have a life of its own, you try to read a newspaper, but you can't focus on the articles. You are already gone; only the announcement of your flight being delayed could stir your emotions up and connect you back with reality. You try to imagine what will be waiting for you when you arrive. It is out of your hands now, you've made the important choice to go, and the world will deliver whatever it has in store for you upon arrival.

As you board your flight, you are accompanied by a crowd of strangers moving across the world for a reason: travel, business, personal affairs, escape. Onward they go. Lives packed tightly in suitcases or trunks or cardboard boxes stamped FRAGILE. HANDLE WITH CARE. Some of them do not feel the magic of the journey, the fact that they are leaving Paris at 3:00 P.M. to reach London at the same 3:00 P.M. They won't think about it, but I marvel at it. I am cheating time; I am getting one hour younger. I am ready to run around the world trying to beat up the timetable and make it an eternal 3:00 P.M. the same day and wherever I go. Departure is a state of sheer pleasure, a unique opportunity to leave everything behind, start anew, and for a moment truly believe that you have total power over the world and your destiny.

Isabelle is a French American and was formerly a journalist in Paris. She is now living in the United States with her husband where they are raising two bilingual boys. Her story was inspired by her personal choice to marry ten years ago and then to leave her country, family, and friends to be with her new husband in the United States.

"Leaving gives you tremendous power. It's some-times hard to make the choice, but then, onward you go, and most of the time it is for the best. Many women feel they don't possess the strength or determination to change their lives. They do."

Simple
Pleasures

Orange Happiness

Joy Harding

It was a few years ago, when all the shoes were so clompy — I had gained some weight that year, too, so I felt even clompier. I was going to lose that weight, but I always seemed to be so hungry.

Anyway, I had stopped at the shoe store next to the grocery store to get a new pair of tennis shoes. My old ones had never seen a tennis court; they were just worn-out from housework. I was debating about whether beige or black tennis shoes would be best this time, when I saw the orange shoes. They weren't tennis shoes, in fact they were hardly shoes at all. There were just two thin leather straps that lay across the front of the foot — that was all. They had such high heels — I hadn't seen heels like that in years.

"That is a beautiful pair of shoes," the clerk said, standing behind me. "Genuine leather, and they're half price. Best buy in the store. Here, sit down and try them on."

"Oh, I don't know. Oh, I guess it won't hurt." Somehow, I felt just like Cinderella trying on the glass slipper. I stood up and walked over to the mirror. My ankles were shaking. I hadn't worn high heels for a long time. Even when I got dressed up, I wore sensible shoes.

These were not sensible shoes. They were wild, sexy, beautiful shoes. And somehow, even with my jeans, when I looked in the mirror — I loved them.

I was surprised when my voice said, "I'll take them." I tried to look nonchalant as I paid the still-outrageous half-price. A voice inside kept saying, Are you out of your mind? Tell the man you forgot, or changed your mind or something, and go get your tennis shoes. But another part of me just said, Shut up. I'll buy these shoes if I want to, and I sailed out of the shoe store feeling marvelous.

As soon as I got home, I put the shoes on. They were wonderfully easy to put on. When I walked, they had a tendency to slip off the same way, but I found that if I curled my toes a little, it seemed to help. I rolled my jeans up to my knees and pirouetted in front of the mirror. The shoes made my ankles look slim, and my varicose veins didn't even show as much.

Then I heard a car turn into the driveway. Oh no, Jim's home, I thought. Suddenly, it was very important to hide the shoes. I whipped them off, crammed them in the box, and looked frantically for somewhere to put them. Finally, I jammed them to the back of the closet.

I tried not to look guilty, and I never mentioned the shoes to Jim — never, to this day.

I glued a patch inside my old tennis shoes, but it curled up and made my toe sore. And pretty soon it fell off. I had to wait two weeks until payday to buy a new pair of tennis shoes.

I don't try on the orange shoes as much as I used to, but once in awhile when I'm searching for something or cleaning the closet, I come across those genuine leather orange shoes. I still think they're beautiful. When I try them on, I stand in front of the mirror and bend my ankle in (like the models in the magazines) and I feel young and slim and happy inside. Then I fold the shoes in the tissue paper and put them back in the closet, and I know that was one of the best investments I ever made.

Every woman needs her own pair of "orange shoes." This little secret of Joy's made her feel young and beautiful, worth every penny of her investment.

Joy helps her husband operate their RV park, a summer resort for retired people. She enjoys writing. "I wrote short stories and poems as a student; then I took twenty years off to help build a business and raise our son. I resumed writing when I started taking classes."

The Front Porch: Why Don't We Use It Anymore?

Vivian Latimer Cropper

Why don't we use our front porch anymore? We do. It has flowers and doormats and doorbells and an entry. But where are the chairs and the people and the laughter? When I was growing up in the forties and the fifties, the front porch was our place to sit, talk, and have a cold drink at the end of the day. Our neighbors came over and we talked about our lives. Kids played and the adults laughed. Perhaps it was the newness of the postwar migration to the suburbs and the return of our mothers to the home and our fathers from the war that spawned this reverie and camaraderie.

Driving down my street now in the summer, I see a few kids out playing, but few adults outdoors. We are not on the front porch talking. We are all in our houses watching television, surfing the Internet, or faxing an order to one of the many catalog companies that barrage our mailboxes each day. A few of us may be reading a book or perhaps listening to our favorite CDs.

We jump into our cars to go to the grocery store, which is only a few blocks away. Our cars and homes have become our seclusion. We have all moved away from the towns where we grew up and where our parents live. Our children see their grandparents at Christmas, if then. We all have two or three telephone lines, or more, so that we can fax, be on the computer, and talk on the telephone at the same time. It is very convenient . . . and cloistered.

I have banked at the same institution since 1970, and yet I do not know one single person that works there anymore. All of my banking is done by night deposit, mail, or through a tube that sucks it inside to a teller that I may talk to but never see. Soon we will be able to do our grocery shopping via a faxed order form and pick it up at a drive-through window, the bill already charged to a credit card. This places me and others one more step out of contact with society. The convenience and timesaving potential for taking care of such mundane tasks in this automated way is very tempting.

My five-year-old grandson has been computer-fluent since he was barely two and a half years old. My son, a physicist and software engineer for a major company, gave his son his own computer when he was barely big enough to reach the keyboard while sitting on a phone book. He learned to read from a program that I gave him long before he started school this year. He spends a great deal of his time playing games on his computer, as well. Although I am very proud of his advanced accomplishments, I would rather get a phone call from him than an E-mail. It would also make my heart glad to hear he was out playing baseball or kick the can with his friends a little more often, rather than sitting in the office with his computer blazing. Computers can't teach him how to get along with people in the real world.

Does the arrival of the information/technological age mean that information is more important than social life? I don't think so. We need information in order to survive, and having it available certainly promotes that end. Human life depends on people communicating with one another through personal interactions, along with age-old learning and tradition within our own cultures. My son had to teach his son certain of his own life experiences before he could attempt the technology of his computer. This type of learning will never be replaced by technology.

I am certainly not antitechnology. I have almost every technological device imaginable in my home office. I cannot imagine surviving in this world without these machines and maintaining any sort of order in my life. My major point in this dialogue is the fear for the younger generation of never fully experiencing one of the most important tenets in life: a diversity of people and ideas. By growing up in a culture secluded behind computers, television screens, and other technology, they may never feel the warmth of the front porch as many of us knew it. The global world of technology is incredible and interesting, but we must not let it remove us from being part of our own villages. Even the person who sits at a computer all day and a television at night should stop and smell the roses that grow on the side of the porch and pet his or her neighbor's dog.

In 1995, Vivian returned to college, and her featured story is extracted from an article written for a class. "I left college in 1963, due to the birth of my son." She believes it is never too late to enjoy life and follow through with a dream, even at fifty-four: "This has been a very important passage in my life, and very fulfilling." Vivian received her bachelor of science degree in sociology in June of 1997 and started graduate school last fall.

Sun and Water

Deelee Roland

The brilliant sunshine reflected upon the swimming pool, highlighting his dark brown eyes and long golden lashes. He looked handsome and strong. I sat staring at him for a moment, almost ready to respond to his requests for me to play — Just one more time — when I stopped myself from acting. We had been playing awhile, and he never seemed to tire of being in the water. I asked him to get out and warm up in the sun. I was worried about him; he'd been either swimming or standing on the steps for more than three hours. He silently gave me a look, as if to say, Make me. After several attempts at trying to catch him, I ventured inside, confident he would be safe because he's an excellent swimmer. There he stood on the steps of the pool, his body shivering and teeth chattering, all the while looking at me through the glass doors. Suppressing the overwhelming feelings of impatience that began to arise in me, I went about my work. Frequently, I found myself in a state of impatience, whether it was while driving, waiting for a return telephone call, or in my relationships. I was my own worst enemy and could easily make myself crazy. My ultimate test in life

. . . patience. I did not need to be anywhere today; yes, I had time to be serene and enjoy life.

It made me smile to think of the many times we had played this game in the past six years, and how often I forgot the way to win. My usual tactic is trying to outsmart him. Instead, I end up chasing my tail around in circles, so to speak. Although he seems quirky, he is far too keen for enticements and trickery. Authority has no bearing and yelling only results in my blood pressure rising. The best approach is to develop a nonchalant attitude and patience, keeping in mind the proverbial "a watched pot never boils."

It is nearly impossible to be mad at him. He's so sweet and lovable and has an array of endearing qualities. Impatience replaces any hint of anger, and I become the neurotic participant, while he looks at me calmly, as if I am the crazy one. I step back and ask myself, What is the big deal? He loves the water — no puddle or body of water is left untouched without at least one splash.

I have found, through the years, the quickest way to get him out of the water, so he doesn't freeze, is to ignore him. Inevitably, this method works, much like it does in the flow of life. Pushing the events of life, trying to force them to happen, slows the process and many times creates a self-induced frustration. I am continually trying to master the "go with the flow" attitude in my career and personal life. When I take a moment to relish the joy of simplicity, I feel radiant, like the sun. When I let events transpire in a natural progression, I become buoyant in the sea of life. I was great at working myself into a frenzy, trying to force or control situations, until I realized the only control I needed was of myself.

In a remote way, I think he knows more about life, and the simple lessons to be learned, than all the rest of us. He's very attuned to the world, perceptive, and smart. I see him smile, curling his lip upward, when I begin this game to get him out of the water. Maybe it's my imagination, and my ability to give him qualities he's perhaps not capable of, but I probably could learn a great deal from his knowledge.

Sun, a big, adorable, loving, and funny golden retriever, has learned to play with my psyche and capture my heart. Rationally, I know he does it out of a self-serving desire to be noticed, played with, and because of his obvious love of the water (he does have webbed feet). Big Sun, or Funny Sunny, as he is sometimes called, has a peaceful soul and undeniable patience, with no apparent disappointments. This quirky dog reminds me to stop and enjoy the abundance of idyllic moments that are there for the taking. Seeing Sun in the water is a reminder to watch my pot less, and smile as I feel the joy of life and peaceful feelings when my patience flows.

Ms. Roland has a Bacheler of Arts in psychology and owns a marketing consulting firm. She lives with her husband, son, and her dog, Sun, in Phoenix, AZ.

Yellow Rain Hat

Marilyn J. Spencer

I walked by the window of a clothing store the other day and did a double take. There, right in the front of a display of rainy-weather gear, was the most perfect little yellow rain hat I ever did see.

Now, I'm a sucker for a yellow rain hat. All my life, it seems, I've wanted one. Way back when I was a second grader, my best friend, Betsy, came to school one day in a yellow rain hat. It was an explosion of sunshine on a gray and drizzly day, and my life was not the same for wanting one, too. Right then and there, I vowed to replace the dumb old rain hat that I had to wear.

I pestered my mother for days and weeks afterward about a yellow rain hat. Every time we went shopping together, I pleaded with her to go looking for one like Betsy's. Mostly, she said no to my "foolishness." But sometimes she would give in, and we would comb all the stores within our range. One time, we found a golden yellow slicker and hat combination, the kind that kindergartners wear, but that wasn't the kind a second grader would want to be seen in. It had to be a lemon yellow hat, like Betsy's. Nothing else would do.

One Saturday, I even talked my dad into driving me over to the big shopping center on the other side of town. Excited and expectant, I dragged him through every store there, until exhaustion forced us to quit.

I never did find one.

Even so, some dreams die hard. I never quite gave up in my heart, and my yearning persisted into my teen years and beyond. Once, I stopped a woman on the street who was wearing a yellow rain hat and asked her where she got it. She said it was old and she didn't remember where she'd bought it. Other times, I'd catch a glimpse of one someplace, but it was always on a person, never in a store.

I don't suppose my granddaughters feel the same attraction to a yellow rain hat that I do. I haven't told them about my weakness. I know there are lots of things they yearn for, though. They have to have this or that kind of jeans, the in kind of footwear, the right amount of bag in their baggy tops, and even socks that exactly match their sweaters. They seem devastated when they can't find what they want. I think it wouldn't do much good for me to tell them there will always be something in life they can't have, that they'll get over it, and that in the long run it won't make much difference. I doubt if they'd believe me anyway.

Maybe you have to be a grandmother to have learned these things. Even if I tried to enlighten those teenagers, so dear to my heart, how then could I explain the presence in my closet right now of a brand-new, perfect little yellow rain hat?

Marilyn decided to write her story when she was looking back on some of her past desires, "so devoutly wished for at the time," and she realized from the distance of a grandmother's wisdom that many of them were unfulfilled. She discovered, "It didn't matter in the long run. I've found a touch of humor goes a long way in acceptance of such truths."

Summer Magic

Jettie M. McWilliams

As a child
I experienced the glory of summer's early dawn,
And the slowly fading shadows at sundown.
I was overflowing with joyous laughter
As I ran and jumped in fanciful play.
And animals joined me at the end of the day.

In my youth
I captured the magic of summer's splendor,
My soul embraced the majestic grace and tender
Enchantment of the summer wind,
The romance of a starlit night.
The days filled with hope and light.

The twilight lingers
The magical moments of summer begin to wane.
My senses remember the melancholy strain
Of music and lost loves in days long past,
The summer magic. Dreaming of yesterday,
I am once again the child at play.

Jettie is a professor emeritus of educational psychology and still enjoys teaching part-time. Her story was prompted by her grandchildren's enthusiasm for life, and how they inspire and remind her of "summer magic" at any age.

The Whole Story

Susan Stirling Meyn

Isn't it funny how stories weave themselves around and pick up pieces of this part of life and that part of life? There isn't any one time that has been separate from another part of my life. It is whole. And that has been my quest, too, to become whole.

I find it difficult winding my way through life's changes. And, like so many other people in today's world, I've had plenty of practice. It is always my current transition that is most difficult, having grieved and grinned over passages long past. I know logically that I survived before and will probably survive again . . . but I'm never sure.

When my children grew up and left, I was, frankly, relieved. I had been a single parent for ten years and was very tired and yearned for some time alone. Who was I really and how could I achieve wholeness? That is what I needed more time to pursue. Of course, I then met a man who, after some struggles and some counseling and a lot of time, did become my husband. But that is getting ahead of my story.

It seemed reasonable to me to want to be in a relationship after my children left. After all, aren't we, as human beings, tuned for partnership? Isn't that our biological urging? I thought my marriage to a man who clearly adored me would round out my life and that I would have years to enjoy my wholeness. Of course that would be too simple.

As soon as I got settled into my sweet marriage, I could really *feel* all of that tiredness and exhaustion rising up from being in charge for all those years before. My husband's job of twelve years disappeared as his company cut back their staff. I was left to continue with my work while my husband created a new business. And I said, "No problem! I know how to support myself!" Of course, that was only partly true. I didn't want to support myself; I thought marriage would allow me some security and relief from the pushing. Apparently, that was not to be.

Time passed. My work became more difficult, less fun, and eventually I lost interest in what I had been doing for fifteen years. I was tired. I wanted to stop but didn't know how else to create income. I am still struggling with this transition, I have not yet reached the other side.

I am learning to do less and be more. My husband supports my changes and the journey we are taking together. He hasn't hassled me about making more money or figuring out where I am going. He has left me alone, and I have been finding my way, one step at a time.

The hardest step in this process is stopping, not pushing, not comparing myself to others and how they are doing. I am slowly learning to stop, listen, breathe, see more clearly, open my heart, and forgive myself more.

The changes within me since I've stopped the pushing have been great but subtle to outsiders. I am learning to work at what I enjoy and what I do well. I have to stop often to make sure I am on track. It is a little disorienting to operate in this fashion after spending a lifetime trying so hard to force things to work. I am now amazed when good things happen, opportunities present themselves, and plans seem just to fall into place.

So I am learning about becoming whole, that is my life's quest. But, I cannot be whole without including everything and everyone around me. To the extent that I can be conscious of all that is around me, I am whole. As I appreciate and care for the earth, its people, and the creatures who inhabit it, I can be whole. But, I cannot try to push my way into completeness. The only way I can catch a glimpse of the heaven that surrounds us is by slowing down and really seeing what is around me. My wholeness is here and beyond me in each moment. I just may find this passage the best one ever.

Susan has helped many others deal with their life transitions in her work as a therapist. "At the time I wrote this story, I was moving into a new phase of my life — I wanted to do more writing and felt this was a tool to express my thoughts. My current journey includes teaching others this kind of tool for self-care and ongoing growth."

Pauses

Sherri Waas Shunfenthal

A great musician was asked what made his piano playing so beautiful. He answered that it was not his playing; it was the pauses between the notes that made the music so lovely.

During a recent thunderstorm, I was busy writing. I had a deadline to finish an article. I am the type of person who carefully plans every day. I always have an eye on what I will do next. However, my youngest son ran out of bed because he was afraid of the storm. I did not want to stop writing, but the two of us went to our big sliding glass doors and watched the storm in the night. It was magnificent the way the tree branches swished and swayed as if they were part of a feverish dance. The sky changed colors as the lightning lit it up. The thunder roared at us. It was amazing.

My son and I held each other tightly. Then my daughter and older son ran out of bed and joined us. I explained to them what causes storms and that sometimes we are afraid of things we don't understand. When my youngest son went to bed, he told me, "I was scared, but when I looked into your eyes and you talked to me, I was not scared." My five-year-old daughter told us, "We are all pieces of a puzzle, the sun, the moon, and all the people, too." It was a magical night with a magical dialogue shared among us. I was glad that I had stopped what I was doing to be with them.

Often my children ask me questions. Then I need to pause to reflect. I do not always know the answers. "How do birds stay in their nest without falling out when there is a storm?" "Who made all the stars in the sky?" "Why aren't there any more dinosaurs?" I pause to reflect for a moment. Then I, too, am filled with the wonder of the world and all the questions to be answered.

When we go walking, we do not walk briskly and get exercise. We walk slowly and stop to admire a spiderweb or a squirrel breaking open a nut. My children suddenly get excited by something I might not notice, like the way grass grows between the cracks of the sidewalk or the way a trail of ants crosses the pavement. They remind me to stop and be in awe of nature.

My children make me pause in what I am doing to give me hugs and kisses. Their soft cheeks next to mine during a harried day make me remember that there is tenderness and goodness in the world.

Yes, my children slow me down. I do not walk as fast when I am with them. They constantly interrupt me. They make me pay attention, and remind me it is the pauses between the busy notes of life that make the music so beautiful.

Sherri is a freelance writer and poet, she has written articles that have appeared in several publications, and her poetry has been published in magazines and books. Her story reminds us to take time out of our busy schedules each day to pause, enjoy life, and "see the world in a fresh, imaginative way."

We hope you have enjoyed this Large Print book. Other G.K. Hall & Co. or Chivers Press Large Print books are available at your library or directly from the publishers.

For more information about current and up-coming titles, please call or write, without obligation, to:

G.K. Hall & Co.
    P.O. Box 159
    Thorndike, Maine 04986 USA
    Tel. (800) 223-2336

OR

Chivers Press Limited
Windsor Bridge Road
Bath BA2 3AX
England
Tel. (0225) 335336

All our Large Print titles are designed for easy reading, and all our books are made to last.